FAILURE:
THE BACK DOOR
TO SUCCESS

FAILURE:
THE BACK DOOR
TO SUCCESS

ERWIN W. LUTZER

MOODY PUBLISHERS
CHICAGO

Unless otherwise indicated, Scripture quotations are from the ESV® Bible (The Holy Bible, English Standard Version®), copyright © 2001 by Crossway, a publishing ministry of Good News Publishers. Used by permission. All rights reserved

Scripture quotations marked NASB are taken from the New American Standard Bible®, Copyright © 1960, 1962, 1963, 1968, 1971, 1972, 1973, 1975, 1977, 1995 by The Lockman Foundation. Used by permission. (www.Lockman.org)

Interior design: Erik M. Peterson
Cover design: Smartt Guys design
Cover and interior photo of open door copyright © 2010 by Auris/iStock (14836411). All rights reserved.

Library of Congress Cataloging-in-Publication Data

Lutzer, Erwin W
        Failure, the back door to success.

1. Success.   2. Failure (Psychology)
3. Psychology, Religious.   I. Title.
BF637.S8L87   158'.1   75-16177
ISBN 978-0-8024-1330-7

2001044967

We hope you enjoy this book from Moody Publishers. Our goal is to provide high-quality, thought-provoking books and products that connect truth to your real needs and challenges. For more information on other books and products written and produced from a biblical perspective, go to www.moodypublishers.com or write to:

Moody Publishers
820 N. LaSalle Boulevard
Chicago, IL 60610

3 5 7 9 10 8 6 4 2

Printed in the United States of America

*To Harry Verploegh, who persistently
reminded me that nothing—
not even our supposed failures or successes—
is as important as learning to
worship the Lord our God*

CONTENTS

FOREWORD

There. Failure is one of the uglies of life. We deny it, run away from it, or, upon being overtaken, fall into permanent paralyzing fear. Probably because of our reluctance to face it, not much is written about the anatomy of failure. As Christians we wave our visionary banners proclaiming, "Victory in Christ," refusing often even to admit that the path to ultimate victory may include intermediate bloody noses.

Accidents on the road to success are, of course, often blamed on the heavy traffic in which we travel. Pastor Lutzer's no-fault insurance plan advises the victim not to criticize other people's or even his own reckless driving so much as to evaluate his collision and move on. The author's route up out of the ditch is paved with common sense, logical reasoning, and biblical authority. Anyone who himself has been stuck in the slough of despond will gratefully respond to this simple escape plan. It bears the stamp of authenticity.

Not only the return road to success but the path to fulfillment is mapped out. Of his own success, Dr. Lutzer says, "I was so busy I scarcely had time to ask God to rubber-stamp my plans!" Success without satisfaction is little reward; learning to follow God's directions adds the mission dimension. It is this component of the book that makes it more than a mere manual for staying inside the solid white line.

Solving problems assumes we ask and answer the right questions: Why failure? How can one change a poor self-image? What happens when a Christian steps out of God's will? Is it ever too late? What does God want most from His children? Through twelve chapters Lutzer delves into the "whys" of the loser syndrome.

With disarming honesty, Lutzer heaves an initial sigh of boredom and frustration with the current spate of success manuals and proceeds with sensitive understanding to show why and how we are so often checkmated. Some of his real-life vignettes stumble right on down to final defeat—just like it happens in experience. The reader instinctively picks up the vibes that this man knows what failure is about.

For the new believer, beset by the many chuckholes of the Christian life, this book is a valuable guide for the journey. For the more experienced Christian, who has as much as sprained his spiritual ankle, it is a welcome support and encouragement. Happily, I think, this writer had avoided the buck-up-and-look-on-the-bright-side counsel. Instead he says, in effect, "Now, son, let's take a look at what's wrong here. Yep, you're right. It's not so good. But you can get out of that booby trap with some know-how. There's a foolproof way. You listen here."

This book is sorely needed in our overanalyzed, under-motivated, and guilt-ridden Christian society. It can be a life changer to anyone tired of the old one-step-forward-and-two-backward routine.

HOWARD G. HENDRICKS

PREFACE

Perhaps you have been as frustrated as I at the many books available on the topic of how to be a success. Many of these books are written for people who simply lack initiative or who haven't established worthy goals for their lives. But there are scores of Christians whose lives are so characterized by perpetual failure that simply applying some novel "secret" of success smacks of mockery.

What about those whose lives are filled with regret? What about those who have committed gross sins? Or those who have been trapped into a meaningless marriage? Where do such people begin in their quest for peace and fulfillment?

My conviction is that failure of some kind is common to us all. And since God had people like us in mind when Christ died, God's grace is adequate to make the best of any situation. Successful people are those who apply God's remedy for failure.

This does not mean that we must fail miserably before we can be a success; it does mean that we cannot be successful in God's sight until we see our own sinfulness—our potential for failure. Only those who see themselves as utterly destitute can fully appreciate the grace of God.

Although personal failure is not a requirement for being a success, our failures can be used as steppingstones to a more meaningful relationship with God. Having failed, we can yet be successful in God's sight because of the incredible generosity of God's forgiveness and acceptance.

This book has been written with the earnest prayer that it might be an encouragement to us as Christians. As I shall explain later, some people who believe they are successes may actually be failures; others who have failed may really be quite successful. For all, there is hope! Salvation was designed for people who have made mistakes, failed, and sinned. Despite our past, all of us can say, "I delight to do your will, O my God" (Psalm 40:8).

CHAPTER 1

FAILURE IS FOR REAL

I didn't know whether to laugh or cry; so I laughed, then I cried."

Discouragement was etched indelibly on Jim's face. He spoke with urgency and only occasionally showed the trace of a smile. "Living for Christ is fine if you are on the top of the pile," he surmised with conviction, "but it's a different story when you are at the bottom."

Two years before this, I had met Jim (not his real name) when he was in high school. He had recently accepted Christ as his Savior. I'll never forget his impromptu prayers. "Lord, it's me again," he'd say. "Remember old Duncan Bell? Well,

You know I don't like him, so I need all the help You can give me."

After high school Jim was accepted for Royal Canadian Mounted Police training in Canada. From the first day, he sincerely tried to be a witness to his comrades. He read his Bible, refused to share sordid jokes, and would not participate in sensual amusements. In short, he "lived for Christ," as most preachers urge us to do.

And that was the beginning of his troubles. Friends dubbed him "the religious nut." Some scorned his piety. Others schemed to have him blamed for activities he did not do. He was ousted (often literally) from the games and social events of his companions.

Perhaps this is what Christians should expect. Are not the godly promised persecution? Did Christ not say that we should rejoice when we are reviled, because our reward would be great in heaven? Yes.

But one fact troubled him. In any group, one person is always first, but by necessity, one must also be last. Jim had that distinction.

He got the lowest score on examinations and barely passed in practical achievements. He was not a leader; neither did he have a winsome personality. Worse yet, he commanded little or no respect.

As we talked together, he stared aimlessly into space. "My friends are rejecting Christ," he commented, "but maybe it's just because they don't want to be like me, and on that score I don't blame them. Who'd want to be like me?" He forced a smile to hold back the tears. "I'm a failure, and I know it."

My mind raced over all those sermons I have heard about how we should do well at school or at our vocations to be a "testimony." But that advice couldn't apply to Jim. God had not given him the ability to gain the respect of others by intellectual or physical accomplishments.

So I explained to Jim—or at least I tried to explain—that maybe God didn't expect as much from him as He did from others. Maybe he should accept his limitations and learn to be satisfied with his role in life. But my explanation was either deficient or unconvincing, or both.

A year later Jim committed suicide.

Shocking? Yes. I did not suspect that Jim had become that discouraged. It was the last desperate act of a Christian who believed that success was forever beyond his grasp.

Since that time I've come to know many who are like Jim. They read the how-to-be-a-success books, they try positive thinking, and yet they are hounded by the suspicion that they are failures.

Most of us have unclear (usually false) notions of success. We hear testimonies of converted movie stars, professional singers, or those who are "successful" in some vocation. Unconsciously, we assume that all Christians should be like them.

Perhaps we have forgotten that not many wise, noble, and mighty are chosen by God. We judge ourselves and others by a false standard.

A *few* noble, wise, and gifted are called. But they are exceptions. God usually chooses the weak, the ordinary, and the despised. Why, then, do so many of us believe we are failures? Perhaps we have a totally *false notion of success.* More of that later.

Many Christians feel trapped because of ugly circumstances. Some have made wrong choices or have been discouraged because they are "out of God's will."

Consider Beth. She accepted Christ at the age of ten.

A dozen years later, she fell in love with a promising young executive. She blissfully entered marriage without a single reservation about her serious-minded husband. *Of course* God would bless their marriage. *Of course* they'd live happily. But optimism does not guarantee success.

For more than twenty years she has lived with a hot-tempered, egotistical, and irrational husband. He rashly punished the children for misdeeds he falsely supposed they committed. He even now demeans his wife in public and is insensitive to her needs. The children are floundering in rebellion, trying to adjust to the world.

Before her marriage Beth sang, played the piano, and displayed other artistic abilities. But these gifts were quickly squelched under the ironhanded rule of a jealous husband. Now most of her life is behind her. She is broken in spirit and weary of life itself. She belatedly asks, "Was my marriage in the will of God? If not, can God ever bless me again? Where does someone begin when it's too late to begin from the beginning?" Is any type of success still open to someone who has been trapped in a senseless marriage?

Such questions can only be resolved by a correct understanding of the will of God. Often we assume that God is unable to work in spite of our weaknesses, mistakes, and sins. We forget that God is a specialist; He is well able to work our failures into His plans.

Finally, there is Brian. He and his wife were accepted for missionary work in Africa. Evidently they had misjudged their ability to adapt to the alien culture of a primitive tribe. Soon after they arrived in Africa they began to resent their new role. They felt it was unfair for them to sacrifice promising careers for people who did not appreciate them. They felt isolated, resentful, cheated.

Had God called them to Africa? It seemed so. They would not have been there if they had not believed that God had led them to missionary work.

That sense of calling had now disappeared. Or, at least, it *seemed* to them that God was not keeping His side of the bargain. They promised to go if He would bless. They went, but there was no blessing.

In order to save face and to give themselves the satisfaction of knowing they were not quitters, they stayed to the end of the four-year term. By that time the conflicts with fellow missionaries and the pressure of the foreign culture had left this young couple emotionally scarred.

When they returned home, their friends anticipated glowing reports about their missionary endeavors. Could they return home, and with a bit of exaggeration, give the reports the people expected? That was one possibility. But how could they explain why they would not be returning to Africa? Would that not belie their glowing reports? No, they preferred to become a statistic, "a missionary casualty." They relocated in a large American city and simply informed their friends that they would not be returning to Africa for "health reasons."

Such an adjustment was both easy and difficult: easy because Brian was able to get a job readily; difficult because they were hounded by the realization that they were failures. Permanently.

No success in America could erase the gnawing fact that they had not been able to survive spiritually in the fierce struggles of cross-cultural adaptation. One thought lodged in their minds: *they were now doomed to be second-class citizens of the kingdom of heaven.*

Furthermore, they found it awkward to pray for God's

blessing. If they were called to Africa and were now out of God's will, could they *sincerely* expect God to bless them? Can God bless those who skirt the hard road and substitute an easy one?

There are thousands of Jims, Beths, and Brians. Some have been forced into marriage by pregnancy; others have faced bankruptcy. Many parents have had to watch their children rebel against Christianity. Countless others are defeated, pessimistic, and guilt-ridden. They are convinced that they will be second-class citizens in the kingdom.

There is another class of failures: those who mistakenly believe they are successes. They may earn an honest living and be fine supporters of the church. They unconsciously (or sometimes all too consciously) consider themselves examples for others to follow. Yet they do not realize that from God's perspective they are failures. One man put it this way: "I climbed the ladder of success only to discover that my ladder was leaning against the wrong wall!"

Heaven will be filled with surprises. Many "successful" Christians will be nobodies, and some whose lives were strewn with the wreckage of one failure after another will be great in the kingdom.

This book is written *for those who believe they are failures and for those who falsely believe they aren't!* It is a message of hope for those who are filled with regret; it is a message designed to disturb those who mistakenly feel they have "made it" in life.

The pages that follow are a modest attempt to rid us of worldly notions of success and humbly return us to God's perspective.

By what standard does God measure success? What happens when we are disobedient? What can we do when it is too late to begin again?

CHAPTER 2

CHOOSING YOUR YARDSTICK

A college student wrote the following letter to her parents:

> *Dear Mom and Dad,*
>
> *Just thought I'd drop you a note to clue you in on my plans. I've fallen in love with a guy called Jim. He quit high school after grade eleven to get married. About a year ago he got a divorce.*
>
> *We've been going steady for two months and plan to get married this fall. Until then, I've decided to move into his apartment (I think I might be pregnant).*
>
> *At any rate, I dropped out of school last week, although I'd like to finish college sometime in the future.*

On the next page, the letter continued,

> *Mom and Dad, I just want you to know that everything*
> *I've written so far in this letter is false. NONE of it is true.*
> *But, Mom and Dad, it IS true that I got a C- in*
> *French and flunked my Math. It IS true that I'm going to*
> *need some more money for my tuition payments.*

This girl made her point! Even bad news can sound like good news if it is seen from a different perspective. Success and failure are relative: their meaning depends on the standard of comparison we use.

Unfortunately, we often judge ourselves and others by inadequate yardsticks. We are quick to compare ourselves with a superficial standard. On this basis, we either conclude that we have "made it" in life, or else we assume the opposite, that we have failed miserably and are beyond hope.

Neither conclusion may be correct. Remember, it's the standard that counts. Let's consider a few common notions of success, all of them distortions that we have borrowed from the world.

COMPARING OUR ABILITIES

Have you ever overheard students discussing the results of their exams? One says, "I got an A"; the other sulks, "He gave me an F."

Human nature? Yes. We tend to blame others for our failures and take credit for our success. Also, we usually use our friends as a basis of comparison.

This is not all wrong, of course. A student should strive for high grades; a Christian businessman ought to succeed financially (and honestly). But often a spirit of comparison breeds envy and discontent.

Consider the man who will not become involved in the church because he feels inadequate. He even might disguise his pride (which lies at the root of all such attitudes) and call it humility. He will convince himself that this feeling of inferiority shows that he is truly humble. Actually, he is so concerned that people think well of him that he will not expose himself to any situation where he can fail. He plays it safe and does nothing.

Parents are often guilty of making their children targets of unfavorable comparison. "Why can't you be like Matt!" they shout with disgust. They forget that no child is *the* standard by which others are to be judged.

God did not make us like General Motors makes Buicks (the only difference is the color and serial number). God did not give everyone the same ability, intelligence, or aptitude. And if we wish to make everyone the same, we are discrediting the wisdom of God. Our abilities (or lack of them) are not an accurate barometer of success or failure.

COMPARING BANKBOOKS

Listen to a conversation in a barbershop or at a Starbucks. You will soon learn that the most popular basis of comparison is *money.* You would think that the chief end of man is to earn money and enjoy it forever!

A wife who compares herself with her friends is tempted to become dissatisfied with her husband's income. She feels cheated because she cannot buy the clothes or furniture her wealthy friends enjoy. She is in bondage to the social status of her neighbors.

If money is a basis of judging success or failure, it is

obvious that Jesus Christ was a failure! Consider this: when He had to pay taxes, He asked Peter to find a coin in a fish's mouth. Why? He didn't have a coin of His own.

Christ was born under the shelter of a stable's roof. Most of us would be appalled if our children could not be born in a modern hospital! When He died, the soldiers cast lots for His garment. *That* was all He owned of this world's goods. He died naked, in the presence of gawking bystanders.

Was Christ a failure? Yes, if money is the standard by which He is judged. The foxes have holes, the birds of the air have nests, but the Son of Man did not have a place He could call home.

Of course, earning money (and even saving some) is both legitimate and necessary. But the amount we earn is not a barometer of God's blessing. The sun rises on the righteous as well as the wicked. In fact, it is usually the wicked who prosper and God's children who are often penniless.

Yet, even Christians (who above all people of the earth should know better) still think they are better (or worse) than others because of the amount they earn! Money does not commend us to God.

Remember the parable of the rich man and Lazarus? Lazarus was a beggar whose body was covered with sores. He and the dogs shared the crumbs that fell from the rich man's table. Later, both Lazarus and the rich man died.

Lazarus was taken to Abraham's bosom; the rich man was confined to Hades. Abraham's rebuke was, "Child, remember that you in your lifetime received your good things, and Lazarus in like manner bad things; but now he is comforted here, and you are in anguish" (Luke 16:25). Money is *not* a valid basis for judging success.

COMPARING FRIENDS

Have you ever met a name-dropper? You will recognize him when you do. He is the man who casually informs you that he met the president of the United States at a luncheon and that he is closely acquainted with outstanding athletes. He calls celebrities by their first name. If he could write a book, he'd entitle it *Ten Famous Men Who Met Me*.

More seriously, we often like to be associated with the "right" people. Our pride is nurtured if we can dine with the famous and be entertained by the wealthy. The fact that God has chosen the poor of this world to be rich in faith and heirs of the kingdom often does not dampen our enthusiasm for celebrities.

However, knowing the greatest men and women does not elevate us one centimeter in the sight of God. The best of men are still sinners. If we take pride in the "greats" of this world, we have a warped view of God's values. He chooses the base, the lowly, and the unknown.

James (the author of the epistle of James) was Christ's half-brother. They grew up in the same home, played together, laughed together, and worked together. After Jesus began His public ministry, neither James nor his other brothers could believe that Jesus was the Messiah. Later, the dramatic events of the crucifixion and resurrection convinced them that they had indeed grown up with the Messiah, the King of Israel.

What an opportunity for James to tell his friends, "I knew Him when . . ." But he never did. Neither in his speech in Acts 15 nor in his letter does James ever allude to the fact that Jesus was his half-brother.

The reasons are simple. Being related to *anyone* (including Christ in the flesh) does not improve one's relationship with God. Furthermore, when James did accept Christ as the

Messiah he did not inherit any special privileges that are not available to all who believe. Before God, every individual is either accepted or rejected on *the same basis.*

God is not impressed with celebrities or those who would like to be. He is impressed by only one man—Christ. And only those who accept Christ by faith receive God's approval.

The point? No person is a success because he (or she) is acquainted with the famous of today; conversely, no one is a failure in the kingdom because his friends were not well known.

In the book of James, worldliness is specifically described as an attitude of personal favoritism. It is seeking the friendship of the rich (and, we might add, the famous) and ignoring the poor (James 2:1–10).

The conclusion? "If you show partiality, you are committing sin and are convicted by the law as transgressors" (James 2:9). Your social status has nothing to do with God's standard of success.

COMPARING RESULTS

A friend of mine who pastored a small church told me how depressing it was for him to attend pastors' conferences. There he would suffer through the reports of the wonderful success of other churches. It seemed that all churches had either doubled in their membership or tripled their income during the preceding year.

His church, on the other hand, was small and had a history of difficulties. It had problems with bitterness, complaining, and factions. On some occasions the pastor was publicly humiliated by irate members. His story (which could be the subject of an entire book) reminds us that carnal Christians can be just as obstinate as worldly pagans.

What did the pastor do? He lived with the abuse. He preached Scripture and taught doctrine. Eventually, a few individuals began to show signs of spiritual growth. In the lives of a handful, there was fruit. But most of the seed fell by the wayside; it was choked by thorns of worldly anxiety or drowned in the slough of resentment.

When I heard the full story, I said, "Roy, I would not have stayed there for a month!" His reply was a rebuke: "I've always wondered if I had love for people. God put me in the most trying situation I could endure. He wanted to teach me how to show love in a place where there was none."

Was he a success? Not if nickels and noses are the measuring sticks! Results *can* be a barometer of God's blessing—but not necessarily.

There is at least one instance in Scripture where God called a man to be a failure—according to human standards. After Isaiah responded to God's call by saying, "Here I am. Send me" (Isaiah 6:8), God gave him a discouraging assignment:

> Go, and say to this people: "'Keep on hearing, but do not understand; keep on seeing, but do not perceive.' Make the heart of this people dull, and their ears heavy, and blind their eyes; lest they see with their eyes, and hear with their ears, and understand with their hearts, and turn and be healed." (Isaiah 6:9–10)

Isaiah was told *in advance* that the people would *not* respond to his ministry. He was to preach only to provide a further reason for God's coming judgment! Obviously, you can't always evaluate a preacher by the number that come forward when he gives the invitation.

I don't mean to imply that statistics are totally irrelevant to success. Those who vehemently object to "numbers" are often the ones who have no numbers to count! In the book of Acts, statistics were a part of the record: three thousand were converted on the Day of Pentecost and another five thousand later. But statistics are not the whole story. Results (even *scriptural* results) are not necessarily a proof of God's blessing.

Remember the Israelites at the water of Meribah? They were impatient with Moses. They had repeatedly accused him of bringing them into the desert to let them die. He had brought them out of Egypt, but he couldn't take them into Canaan. Tempers flared. The people felt cheated.

God told Moses to speak to the rock. He, in a fit of anger, hit the rock instead. Yet water flowed! The children and cattle had cool, clear water.

Perhaps a small minority said, "Moses disobeyed. He will be punished." Yet possibly the majority responded, "Why complain? Aren't you glad that we have water? Who cares how it got here. At least we will not die of thirst!"

Water flowed. The people were jubilant. Was Moses a success? Yes, *in the eyes of men. No, in the eyes of God.* His disobedience brought water, but it also brought punishment.

Results in themselves are not a proof that God is pleased. It is possible to win attendance contests and disseminate the gospel and see results; all these activities can be done without pleasing God! Such results can be achieved by deceptive gimmicks or for purely personal satisfaction. It is not enough to do God's work; it must be done in His way and for His credit.

Was Jeremiah a success? Was John the Baptist? Christ? Not by purely human standards. If these men had turned in annual reports, they would not have received achievement awards.

Are *you* achieving results? If so, thank God. If not, take

heart! You might not be as great a failure as you think.

When Christ was on earth He predicted that someday Peter would have his hands stretched out and someone else would clothe him and carry him where he did not wish to go, that is, to his martyrdom. When Peter heard this, he was distressed. He wondered what would happen to his friend John. Would he live until Christ returned, or would he die a horrible death, too? Peter asked, "Lord, what about this man?"

Christ replied, "If it is my will that he remain until I come, what is that to you? You follow me!" (John 21:21–22).

If God wishes to bless others more than us, if they are famous and we are unknown, if they are wealthy and we are poor, if they are gifted and we are mediocre—what is that to *us?* Christ says to us individually, *"You follow Me!"*

A spirit of comparison is worldly, carnal, and devilish. Read carefully Paul's words: "Not that we dare to classify or compare ourselves with some of those who are commending themselves. But when they measure themselves by one another and compare themselves with one another, they are without understanding" (2 Corinthians 10:12).

As Christ would say, *"You follow Me!"*

THE SINGLE EYE

What made Moses a great servant of God? Maybe it was his faith. Perhaps it was patience. I'd like to suggest that it was his humility. When God told him he could not enter the land and Joshua would replace him, Moses showed no trace of jealousy. We might have expected him to say, "Why should this young upstart do in three days what I couldn't do in forty years?" But he didn't. Instead he prayed for God's blessing on his young successor.

Why was Moses not jealous? Because he did not compare his *career with someone else's*. If God wanted to use Joshua in a spectacular way, fine.

Think of this: Christ left the eternal glory of the Father to suffer the ultimate humiliation of a shameful *human* death. Yet He never complained because He had to abandon the glory that the other two members of the Trinity retained. If He had compared His role in redemption with those of the Father and the Holy Spirit, He might have felt cheated. Why should He—equal with the other two members—be the one to become the scum of the earth?

If Christ had compared Himself with other men (remember, He was fully human), He might have thought that He should be the greatest of them. Yet (incredibly) He became the lowest of them. When the disciples were wondering who would perform the duties of a household servant, Christ took a towel and basin of water and washed their feet!

How could the One who was so high stoop so low? One reason is that He did not compare Himself with others but *cared only about meeting the standard that the Father had ordained.* "I delight to do your will, O my God" (Psalm 40:8). That's all that mattered.

Is it realistic for us to follow His example? John the Baptist came close to it. Large crowds had gathered to hear John speak. He generated so much excitement that a special synagogue delegation came to ask him who he was. Some thought he was the Messiah. John was not flattered.

Later, the large crowds left John and began to follow Christ. John's disciples were concerned about their leader's reputation. They did not want their teacher left in the cold.

John was not concerned. He responded, "A person cannot receive even one thing unless it is given him from heaven"

(John 3:27). When one person is more effective than another, it is because God has ordained it so! All abilities and talents are gifts of God. Jealousy in the Body of Christ is an ugly sore, a malignant tumor.

John continued (v. 28), "You yourselves bear me witness, that I said, 'I am not the Christ, but I have been sent before him.'" John evaluated his ministry from a proper perspective. He did not say that he was useless (as those with a false humility are apt to assert). He realized that He was sent before the Messiah but that he himself was not the Messiah. He had a realistic self-image.

In the Middle East, it was customary for the friend of the bridegroom (today we call him the best man) to be sure that no one went into the room of the bride except the proper lover, that is, the bridegroom. The friend of the bridegroom stood by the door so that only the bridegroom could enter. Therefore, the bridegroom would have to identify himself, usually by speaking a few words.

John, using this imagery, told his disciples, "The friend of the bridegroom, who stands and hears him, rejoices greatly at the bridegroom's voice. Therefore this joy of mine is now complete" (John 3:29). John said that his responsibility was merely to introduce the bride to the bridegroom, that is, to introduce Israel to Christ.

John's joy was not found in the crowds. He was not elated because some people mistook him for the Messiah. His satisfaction was found in knowing Christ. And *any* part he could have in introducing people to Christ was neither too great nor too small.

His reputation was not threatened when his ministry was eclipsed by someone greater than he. He could watch his popularity plummet in the wake of another's ministry; there was no jealousy, only joy. In his words, "He must increase, but I must decrease" (John 3:30).

Is such humility unrealistic? John the Baptist was a great man; he could afford to be humble! Christ said that among those born of women there had not arisen anyone greater than John the Baptist. Perhaps if *we* were that great, we would also be that godly. Perhaps if we had known Christ personally as John did, we could accept the end of our career!

Would you like to be as great as John the Baptist? You *can* be. Regarding John, Christ added, "Yet the one who is least in the kingdom of God is greater than he" (Luke 7:28). How do we become great (so secure that we need not compare ourselves with others)? By becoming so small that comparison becomes ridiculous! The least is the greatest; the last shall be first.

Are you ready for the implications of this?

CHAPTER 3

WE'RE ALL CHIPS OFF THE SAME BLOCK

Most of us would agree that success and failure are poles apart. What could be more obvious than the fact that some people "make it" in life and others don't?

After all, the differences among people are striking: there are the rich and the poor, the beautiful and the ugly, the winsome and the boring.

But God isn't impressed with such distinctions. His ways are not our ways; He does not see us as others do.

For this reason we cannot as Christians easily classify ourselves (or others) as either a success or failure. There is a mixture of *both* in us all. In fact, it is only as we understand failure and accept it that we discover the secret of success.

Often the doorway to success is entered through the hallway of failure. Our sins are a forcible reminder of our need for God's grace; our weaknesses make us appreciate God's strength. An understanding of our frailty is the basis for a dynamic relationship with God.

That is why the distinction between success and failure is so slight: the line that divides the two is incredibly fine—so fine that we cannot even recognize it unless we know what we are looking for. More of that later.

Let's back up for a moment and see ourselves as God sees us—whether this flatters us or not. His X-ray shows the following results: *there is not much difference between us.* We are all chips off the same block—Adam. In one sense we are all the same. Let me explain.

OUR NATURES ARE IDENTICAL

Who is the most wicked man that ever lived? Hitler? Eichmann? Judas? Take your choice. His nature at birth was no more wicked than yours. We are *all* the children of wrath (Ephesians 2:3); we are *all* conceived in sin. There is none righteous, *no, not one.*

Read carefully the words of Christ: "For from within, out of the heart of man, come evil thoughts, sexual immorality, theft, murder, adultery, coveting, wickedness, deceit, sensuality, envy, slander, pride, foolishness" (Mark 7:21–22). This description does not merely apply to your neighbor. Christ was speaking about *you.* The potential for every imaginable evil lies within us all.

If that isn't startling, listen to this: "The heart is deceitful above all things, and desperately sick; who can understand it?" (Jeremiah 17:9). In what way is the heart deceitful above all else? It is deceitful because we convince ourselves that we are not really wicked! We tell ourselves that we, by nature, are better than murderers and adulterers. But God knows better. Some people commit greater sins than others; but, by seeing the heart, God knows that the differences between us are negligible. Our sinful natures are essentially the same.

OUR NEW NATURES ARE IDENTICAL

What happens when we believe in Christ? We become a new creation; we receive a new nature. The sinful nature remains, but the new nature is now also within us. All who believe in Christ receive the same nature and the same Holy Spirit. On that score we are identical.

Since we have *both* natures within us, conflict is inevitable. "For the desires of the flesh are against the Spirit, and the desires of the Spirit are against the flesh, for these are opposed to each other, to keep you from doing the things you want to do" (Galatians 5:17). As Christians, we now find that there are spiritual victories—freedom from sins; and also spiritual failures—the times when we lapse back into our former ways. All Christians know this conflict to some degree. We have all experienced a mixture of failure and victory.

Have you heard the story of the two men trying to jump across a thirty-foot river? One jumps ten feet and the other jumps twenty. One does better than the other, but *neither* makes it to the other shore.

This story is usually told to illustrate that only small differences exist between unsaved men. Some are better than others, but everyone is condemned because all come short of God's standards. But this story applies to Christians with equal force.

We have the same sinful nature; we have the same Holy Spirit. We all experience failure of one kind or another. God knows our frame; He remembers that every one of us is dust.

In fact, even those who are considered outstanding Christians and those who are considered failures may not be as far apart in God's eyes as we think.

Let's find out why.

ONLY GOD KNOWS FOR SURE

Our judgments are often superficial. We look at some Christians and are convinced that they are successful in their relationship with God. They have a kind spirit, appear to be happy, and trouble no one. They are generous with their money and do not mind helping fellow believers. Then we look at others who are discouraged or emotionally crippled. Perhaps they are pessimistic and defeated. We are tempted to suggest that the former group is a success and the latter is a failure.

Are such judgments valid? Perhaps yes. More often, no.

Consider this: *the reason some people are more noticeably a success than others is that they have not had a chance to fail!* For example, I have never had to return home defeated from missionary work in a foreign country. But perhaps the reason is that I have never *gone* as a missionary to a foreign country! Can I honestly understand the loneliness, culture shock, and adjustments some missionaries have had to make?

It is cowardly to judge others when they fail to reach goals that we have never tried to achieve ourselves. Spectators find it easy (and enjoyable) to boo a football player for misjudging a play. But what if those spectators had to play? How would they measure up against the skills of that "despicable" quarterback? There is one sure way of never missing a touchdown pass: *just never play the game.*

Think of those who have experienced emotional or mental trauma. Can we honestly understand the pressures they have had to face? Often such Christians have been reared in broken homes, rejected by their parents. Others have had to cope with mental limitations or physical handicaps. Perhaps they do find it difficult to trust God; perhaps they have not yet worked through the resentment that has been nurtured by the harsh environment of a hate-filled family. Are they successful? Let God judge. I, for one, believe that under similar conditions I would have fared no better than they.

Similarly, there are those who have been guilty of overt moral sins. Others have lived in sexual purity. But might it not be that some have not committed adultery because they have not been confronted with explicit moral temptation? Some Christians have been sheltered from the enticement of a Potiphar's wife. Others have grown up in a generation with less moral perversion and fewer temptations.

This is not to suggest (as some might erroneously conclude) that we are not responsible for our sins or that we can simply blame our circumstances if we commit sin. Far from it! Paul did not condone any form of sexual impurity in the church at Corinth, even though such sins were rampant in the city. The Scriptures are filled with warnings, exhortations, and condemnations for those who practice evil.

The fact that circumstances need not force us into sin is vividly illustrated by the story of Joseph. He had every opportunity to commit adultery and get away with it, but he refused to do "this great wickedness and sin against God"

(Genesis 39:9). One of the most powerful indicators of God's power is that He is able to preserve believers from the sins of an adulterous and sinful society.

My point is simply that when we judge others (and it is legitimate to reprove those who have been overcome with a fault or need church discipline), we must do so realizing that we ourselves could easily be guilty of the same sins. If we are free from guilt, it is because of God's grace; it is not because we are inherently better than others. He that believes he is standing should take heed lest he fall! *You and I are capable of indescribable evil. The potential for every sin lies within us.*

Some others never dabble in the lusts of the world because they don't have the nerve! They appear to be successful, but they are not. What keeps them in line is fearing that failure would ruin their reputation.

Remember the elder brother in the story of the prodigal son? Although he is usually ignored (the prodigal receives all the attention), we shall consider the elder brother the focal point of the story. In many ways, he was an example for others to follow. He was a hard worker and lived a "separated" life. While his young brother was enjoying the far country, the elder brother was faithful at home.

Yet, for all this, the elder brother did not please his father. One reason is that the father delighted in giving, and the elder brother refused to accept the father's wealth. Not once did the boy ask for a young goat so that he could enjoy a party with his friends. He refused to accept his inheritance.

A second reason the elder brother did not please the father is that his heart was not in the father's work. His mind was in the far country. He told his father, "When this son of yours came, who has devoured your property with prostitutes, you killed the fattened calf for him!" (Luke

15:30). How did he know his brother had wasted money on prostitutes? He didn't. But the elder brother knew what *he* would be doing if he had a chance to leave the farm! His work was on the farm; his heart was in the far country.

Here was a man busy in the father's work yet out of harmony with the father's heart. This nice boy stayed home only because he didn't have the nerve to leave! His reputation was at stake.

Does this story ring a bell? Unfortunately, many Christians (who appear successful) envy those who enjoy worldly pleasures. They are faithful in church, not because their heart is in it but because they are expected to be involved. The "work of the Lord" is not a delight: it is drudgery. But they know they should not enjoy the world, so they play it safe. They are not failures in their works, but they are failures in their hearts. And the tragedy is that they believe they are fine Christians!

Remember Christ's words? To look at a woman in lust is adultery, and to hate your brother is to be a murderer. And if you *love* the world (even if you do not do worldly things), the love of the Father is not in you.

Of course, overt acts of sin have greater consequences than sins of the heart. In that sense, all sins are not equal. If David had only lusted after Bathsheba instead of committing the act of adultery, the consequences that followed his sins would not have occurred. But *legally* and *judicially* sins of the mind and overt acts are the same in God's sight.

The reason we think there are great differences between Christians is that we compare our lives with those of other believers. When we compare ourselves with God, those differences are negligible. One molehill is nearly the height of another, if you measure them all against the Himalayas.

When God judges us, He takes everything into account. He knows our personal struggles, pressures, and background. He knows all of our failures—public and private. Against the backdrop of God's holiness, we all come far short of God's standard.

Consequently, some Christians who are publicly active in God's work only appear successful *to us*. God judges the heart. Remember, the differences between us are smaller than we care to admit!

Perhaps you think of yourself as a success, or maybe you believe you have failed miserably. Regardless of your opinion, here is good news: God can turn your failures into success if you learn to apply His remedy.

But, before we consider God's plan in detail, we must analyze failure more specifically. What is failure, anyway? What is its cause?

We'll discuss these questions in the next chapter.

CHAPTER 4

A PROFILE OF FAILURE

Intelligent, gifted, well adjusted—all of these descriptions applied to a young man who began his career with every advantage imaginable. He did not have the physical and moral defects that inflict so many of us. He could blame neither his heredity nor his environment if he made unwise decisions. Yet, for all this, there was one other word that described him: *failure.*

This man, more than any other, provides a case study on failure. With virtually all the cards stacked in his favor, he blew an unprecedented opportunity. He could have gone down in history as a hero; but he is remembered primarily for a gigantic mistake: he opened the door for every failure imaginable. Generations of his descendants—in fact, all of us—felt the repercussions of his sin. This man's failure became the basis for our failure; a study of his experience is basically a study of ourselves. The effect of his foolish choice gives the clue to two questions that plague us: What is failure? and, Why do we fail?

The man's name is Adam. He was created perfect by a direct act of God. He was put in a beautiful garden and given a wife. He, for one, did not have to question whether he had married "the right one." At least *that* marriage was made in heaven. Furthermore, he had direct communication with God.

There was no static on the line when he spoke with the Almighty. But Adam failed.

Notice this: Adam was created to have three relationships.

First, he was made in the image of God, so that he would be able to know God (Genesis 1:27). This also involved ruling the earth under God's direction (Genesis 1:26). He would get his orders from God and spend time in fellowship with Him. In this way, Adam would be fulfilling the chief purpose of his existence. It was a great relationship.

Second, Adam was given a wife. He was essentially a social being and needed companionship. The desire for marriage and the need for friends are inherent in us all. A relationship with God does not vitiate our need for one another. God did not create Adam without desires. Since he needed companionship, God saw that he got it.

Third, Adam was adjusted to the world. He was given a garden to cultivate and keep (Genesis 2:15). Taking care of this responsibility was one way of showing his appreciation to God.

Let's suppose that a rich man asked you to oversee his estate. You'd want to be sure that you carried out his orders carefully. You'd also know that everything you cared for was not your own. If it did belong to you, you could do as you wished. But you are responsible to him, because it is his. Similarly, Adam was to take care of God's garden, trees, and animals. He was to submit to God's authority over all creation.

Imagine! Adam was given a job with explicit instructions; he could discuss his work with God; he had a wife that was custom-made. But he failed. He and his wife disobeyed God's direct command that they should not eat of the tree of "the knowledge of good and evil" (Genesis 2:17).

The result? Failure was no longer a mere possibility; it was now a damning reality.

THE COMPONENTS OF FAILURE

What happened when Adam and Eve sinned? The relationships created in the Garden of Eden were destroyed or at best perverted. The three basic drives were still there, but their expression became debased. Now the three legitimate desires were inverted and warped.

We have inherited the consequences of Adam's disobedience. Of course, we also add our own sins to his; by nature we choose to turn away from God. But Adam's sin shattered man's original relationships, and we have been trying to fit the pieces together ever since.

The Bible specifies what the symptoms of these consequences are. John wrote, "For all that is in the world, the lust of the flesh and the lust of the eyes and the boastful pride of life, is not from the Father, but is from the world" (1 John

2:16 NASB). These three expressions describe our perverted drives. Let's consider them one at a time.

First, there is the *pride of life*—self-exaltation. Instead of obeying God, we by nature want to be our own god. Adam chose to eat of the forbidden fruit precisely because he wanted to be like God; he wanted to be his own god. Whenever we substitute our own desires for God we are guilty of pride.

Visualize a young executive as he nervously paces the floor while waiting for an elevator. He is dressed well and knows it. He is secretly pleased with himself. He considers himself superior to others and is determined to force others to admit that "obvious" truth. He is so consumed with ambition that he is almost oblivious to coworkers who walk by. At any given moment he might be filled with resentment toward another man in his company who tried to "cross him." Before he eventually falls asleep at night, he schemes to get even with his rival. In the morning he enjoys a replay of the malicious thoughts of the night before. He can hardly wait to execute his plans.

At home his wife may be starving for companionship. Yet he is so preoccupied with himself (he would say with his *business)* that he runs roughshod over the feelings of his family. He is insensitive to the needs under his own roof. He honestly sees nothing wrong with his lifestyle. Doesn't he provide for his family? Doesn't one have to earn a living? His pride blinds him to the deep emotional and spiritual needs of others.

His wife may be controlled by a different form of pride. Her lifestyle is different from his, and she may even resent her husband's conceit. But she, too, may be the victim of pride—pride that has become complex; it will often turn inward and become an inferiority complex. The symptom of such a psychological attitude is usually depression.

Let me explain. When we withdraw from others, it is usually because of the fear of failure. We often don't want to risk friendship lest someone find out what we are really like. In order to keep our reputation intact, we are tempted to spend our time on the sidelines. Our excuse is inferiority, but the root of it is pride.

Or, let us suppose that we cannot accept ourselves for what we are. The resentment we feel toward others often becomes directed toward ourselves. "Why can't I be like (insert friend's name here)? Why do I have so many handicaps? I was born stupid!" All such attitudes lead to depression, but beneath it all is pride. We are envious of others and angry for not getting the recognition we crave.

Pride in all of its forms is probably the most obvious reason for failure. One person may not be able to work with others because of his stubborn desire to maintain his "rights." Another may resent his colleague's superior ability. Still another may refuse to become involved because of feelings of inferiority. Insensitivity, resentment, and anger—these are symptoms of the "boastful pride of life." All of this started when Adam chose to be his own god.

Second, there is the *lust of the flesh*—the craving for sensual desire. God had given Adam a wife; this relationship defined the prescribed limits of sexual conduct. But, in every age, God's restrictions have been largely ignored. Our own day is characterized by hedonism—the love of pleasure. The sexual revolution has made sexual purity a rarity, if not an oddity. Since "everybody is doing it," the temptation to capitulate to sexual looseness is powerful. Yet, of all sins, sexual immorality is one of the most serious.

Many people—Christians as well as non-Christians—

have succumbed to illicit sexual relationships. Many have had their reputations ruined; some have had their marriages destroyed. As I shall point out later, even in such cases all is not lost. Fellowship with the living God is still always a possibility. But, if pride is the most universal cause of failure, surely sensuality has the most devastating consequences.

The lives of David and Samson in the Old Testament point to this fact: sexual sins have far-reaching repercussions.

Finally, there is the *lust of the eyes*—covetousness. Adam was supposed to work in the garden while recognizing that it belonged to God. God was the owner of all things. If God gave Adam a job to do, he was to be merely a steward. Adam was accountable because he owned nothing.

Today we covet the things of this world—things that belong to God alone. Covetousness is the hallmark of the sales industry. To be content with what we have is a cardinal sin; if we are satisfied with our present car, we will not get a new one. So we are bombarded with advertisements designed to make us dissatisfied with our old phone, our outdated lapels, and our favorite mouthwash.

Many people have an inner compulsion to possess everything they see. If their relatives have better TVs, newer cars, or more expensive homes, they are dissatisfied with their lot in life. Such people are failures because they have invested in the bank of the world—a bank that is already in the red.

What causes failure? What makes a man come to the end of his life and admit he lived in vain? What motivates a man to commit suicide because he is not as gifted as others? What makes a missionary return from Africa because he felt his abilities were unappreciated? What causes a man to jeopardize his Christian testimony and have an affair with his neighbor's wife? The answer: sin—

specifically pride, covetousness, or sensual desire.

Of course, there are failures quite unrelated to sinful motivations: a student might fail in school, or a man might make an unwise investment. Many people have failed at their jobs or simply fallen short of their goals. We shouldn't minimize this type of failure, but in the long run it is not as serious as spiritual failure. God does not expect everyone to have a college education; He did not create us with the capacity to successfully tackle every situation. All of us have at some time set unrealistic goals for ourselves or attempted projects beyond our abilities. These failures usually don't happen because of sin per se but are the result of our lack of ability. Human frailty is ever with us.

However, God often uses this kind of failure to remind us how desperately we need Him. I know of a man who, as a non-Christian, cried to God for help only after his business went bankrupt. A student who flunked college was forced to accept his limitations, and he learned to find his personal fulfillment in God.

My point is this: God is adequate for all kinds of failure. Some failures may not be our fault, but they serve as reminders that we must live with eternal priorities in mind. Other failures are directly the result of our own sinful choices.

This book is primarily concerned with spiritual and moral failure for one reason: these kinds of failure have the most devastating consequences. Flunking school or losing a job is minor in comparison to being controlled by pride, covetousness, or sensual desire. Failures that result from human frailty have no eternal consequences (unless we respond to them in the wrong way). Spiritual and moral failures often permanently affect our children, our friends, and, of course, ourselves. These crushing experiences bring guilt, defeat, and depression. If we know how to apply God's remedy to these spiritual problems, we will find it much easier to accept other kinds of failure.

Did God provide a remedy for the most ugly kind of failure? The answer is yes. He has the wisdom to take the messes we have made and straighten them out. No one has failed too greatly or too often for God. Remember, He had sinners like us in mind when He initiated His redemptive plans.

A PREVIEW OF GOD'S REMEDY FOR FAILURE

God is well aware of the pitfalls along our path. Sin did not take Him by surprise. Long before Adam and Eve were created, God planned to turn our failure into success. With a detailed knowledge of all the facts, God provided a remedy that would not fail—if it was seriously applied.

God's plan is to strike at the root of our problem. He did not decide merely to help us adjust to our misery; we needed something more drastic. Furthermore, his remedy had to be inclusive; it had to be broad enough to cover every eventuality.

If His plan could work only for those with many natural abilities, it would hardly meet the deepest needs of the majority of us. If only those who had committed small sins were eligible to receive the benefits of God's remedy, then God's foresight could be questioned.

Only a God who knows all things and who has infinite wisdom could draft a plan that would anticipate virtually every situation, every sin, every failure. God has done just that.

The focal point of the plan is Christ's death on the cross. That sacrifice made forgiveness for all sins a possibility. Thus, broken communication between us and God can be repaired.

God can again be loved, obeyed, and worshiped. Forgiveness in its fullest sense can be a reality.

Furthermore, God intends to change our basic motivations. We need not be controlled by pride, covetousness, or lust. Christ's death did not only make forgiveness possible; it also opened the door to a life of personal freedom from the sins that plague us. But, before we can enjoy such a new relationship, we have to face our sin squarely. Many people who ask for God's help are disappointed. The reason? They should begin by asking for God's forgiveness. Asking for God's strength before we have confessed our weaknesses (sins) is like trying to cure a headache with a Band-Aid. God wants to go to the root of our problem. Once we understand how sinful we are, we will appreciate God's grace.

My purpose in the succeeding chapters is to concentrate on how God can take our failures, forgive them, and then incorporate us back into His plan. Even those who are entangled in a web of sin can still find acceptance and fulfillment with God.

What is failure? It is living with perverted values. It is being hooked on one or more of the three worldly motivations.

What is success? It is learning to apply the grace of God. It is understanding how we can be accepted by God despite our bitter experiences in the past.

GOD'S DEFINITION OF SUCCESS

Some people please God, and others do not. We cannot judge, for our knowledge is superficial. Our basis of judgment is often wrong. We are "outward" oriented; God is "inward" oriented.

If success is learning to apply God's grace, how do we

49

do this? The first step is to stop trusting ourselves and to trust Christ alone for our acceptance before God. Then, God declares us righteous despite our personal failures. The implications of this will be discussed later. The key question you should face now is whether you are depending on your own goodness or trusting the forgiveness God offers in Christ.

Christ illustrated this point with a parable:

> Two men went up into the temple to pray, one a Pharisee and the other a tax collector. The Pharisee, standing by himself, prayed thus: "God, I thank you that I am not like other men, extortioners, unjust, adulterers, or even like this tax collector. I fast twice a week; I give tithes of all that I get." But the tax collector, standing far off, would not even lift up his eyes to heaven, but beat his breast, saying, "God, be merciful to me, a sinner!" (Luke 18:10–13)

Christ's conclusion was, "I tell you, this man went down to his house justified, rather than the other. For everyone who exalts himself will be humbled, but the one who humbles himself will be exalted" (Luke 18:14).

The Pharisee depended on his own works to gain approval before God. But notice carefully: his works were *good*; furthermore, *he thanked God* that he was not like other men. Perhaps this Pharisee did *not* take the credit for his works; he realized that his ability to do good was a gift of God. Yet, even such an attitude doesn't make us acceptable to God!

The tax-gatherer never listed his achievements. Perhaps it was because he never had any; perhaps he realized that even if he did have accomplishments, they could never be acceptable to God.

Therefore, he prayed, "God, be merciful to me, a sinner!" The word *merciful* is more accurately translated "propitious." He prays that God's wrath would be mercifully turned away. As we know, that was later done by the sacrifice of Christ.

The one man went home justified, that is, acceptable to God, the other did not. What made the difference? One realized that his acceptance before God depended solely on God's grace (made available by an offering for sin); the other believed it depended on himself. And *that* separates the successful from the unsuccessful in God's sight.

Notice how clearly the Scriptures teach that our works cannot make us righteous in God's sight. "By works of the law no human being will be justified in his sight, since through the law comes knowledge of sin" (Romans 3:20). And again, "For by grace you have been saved through faith. And this is not your own doing; it is the gift of God, not a result of works, so that no one may boast" (Ephesians 2:8–9). Do you want to have God's approval? You must stop trusting yourself and consciously transfer your trust to Christ. God's standard is so high that only Christ can meet it. So we cannot depend on ourselves but must depend on Christ, who met God's requirement for us. When we decide to trust Christ, God declares us righteous. We are acquitted of our guilt and have God's approval.

But there is a second step to learning to apply God's grace: personal experience. Although our faith in Christ makes us members of God's family, we can dishonor our relationship. The prodigal son had all the rights of sonship; but, when living in a pigsty, he was hardly a credit to his father!

Believing on Christ makes us joint heirs with Him, but we can still choose to live selfish, worldly lives. Legally, we have an incredible spiritual inheritance at our disposal, and our acceptance is secure; but we can fail to accept what God wants to do for us.

So, although as Christians we are all successful in the sense that we have God's unconditional acceptance, we may be *un*successful in experiencing the implications of that acceptance. Consequently, failure—serious failure—is a possibility for us all. Even the apostle Paul feared that, after he had run the race of life and preached to others, he himself should be disqualified (1 Corinthians 9:27).

God wants us to be successful in applying His remedy to our sinful, human condition. This means much more than simply going to church, praying, reading the Bible occasionally, and staying out of trouble. Aren't these things commendable? Yes, even necessary. But an atheist could do as much!

It is wrong to assume that every act of service automatically pleases God. Some Christians refer with smug satisfaction to many years of "faithful service" to the Lord. They are quite sure that they will receive a great reward at the judgment seat of Christ—and, candidly, they believe they deserve it. Obviously, they have not understood the words of Christ that the first shall be last and the last shall be first. Surprises lie ahead!

What then makes our works pleasing to God? It is when they are spiritual sacrifices acceptable to God by Jesus Christ (1 Peter 2:5). That means that even the works of Christians do not inherently please God. Works are pleasing to God only when they are done with the motivation and strength that Christ can give. They are acceptable *by Jesus Christ*.

We've already seen that many appear successful only because they have lived "normal" lives. Some have never had a chance to fail. They have lived respectful and decent lives. Such are often admired in the Christian community, but in

God's sight they are failures: their works will go up in smoke. Why? They lived decently but not supernaturally. They did not have the humility to see how desperately they needed God. Perhaps they thought that their good works gave them special status with God. They did not realize that only Christ has special status with God. We, therefore, are pleasing to God to the extent that we apply God's grace to every experience of our lives.

On the other hand, many who have failed miserably are usually good candidates for appreciating God's grace and power, the most successful discovery a sinner can make. It is not necessary to fail before we succeed, but God often uses our failures to make us more sensitive to our need of Him.

Remember the story of the harlot who brought an alabaster vial of perfume and anointed Christ's feet and then wiped His feet with her hair? As she displayed her love, her tears mingled with the perfume on Christ's feet. When Simon objected, Christ replied,

> Do you see this woman? I entered your house; you gave me no water for my feet, but she has wet my feet with her tears and wiped them with her hair. You gave me no kiss, but from the time I came in she has not ceased to kiss my feet. You did not anoint my head with oil, but she has anointed my feet with ointment. Therefore I tell you, her sins, which are many, are forgiven—for she loved much. But he who is forgiven little, loves little.
> (Luke 7:44–47)

The one who is forgiven much loves much; the one who is forgiven little loves little. The secret of loving Christ—and serving Him acceptably—is to appreciate His forgiveness. It is to live in constant appreciation of God's grace.

No, we don't have to commit gross sins to appreciate God's grace; any sin is vile enough, if we see it in perspective. But many of us are blinded by self-righteousness. We love little, because we *think* we have been forgiven little! The greatest obstacle to applying God's grace is satisfaction in our own accomplishments. A person satisfied with himself never learns to lean on God.

Christ repeatedly taught His disciples this general principle: the last shall be first, the first last. The one who is least realizes that he has nothing to offer God; he comes solely on the basis of God's mercy. He who wishes to be first in the kingdom betrays his belief that he is inherently better than someone else, and because of that deception he will be last!

The result? The humble (who see clearly their need for mercy) are exalted; the proud (who believe they have a slight edge on others) will be brought down.

What then is success? On one level it is receiving Christ as Savior and thereby having His righteousness attributed to us. However, on the level of personal experience, it is living supernaturally; it is living in dependence on Christ. It is being motivated to serve Christ out of sheer gratitude. It is dying to our personal ambitions and letting Christ be in control. To such, Christ will say, "Well done."

The point? From God's perspective, a successful person is one who *knows how to accept God's remedy for failure.* Since we are essentially the same, only an application of God's grace distinguishes us. Let's consider that now.

CHAPTER 5

HOW MUCH CAN GOD FORGIVE?

I can't come to God about *that* sin again," sighed the disillusioned young man. "God is weary of hearing me ask forgiveness for the same thing over and over. I've decided to let everything slide until I know I can hold out." His story is one that in principle has happened a thousand times. He accepted Christ as Savior at about the age of twelve. After the novelty wore off, his relationship with God took a nosedive. During his teen years, he rebelled against his parents' restrictions. He soon learned to swear, drink, and read pornography on the sly. He often asked God's forgiveness and vowed that he would not repeat the endless cycle of personal failure, but for some reason he never made a clean break.

As he grew older, he felt so discouraged that he often would go for days or weeks without praying. Sometimes he determined to do better. He felt sure that if he read the Bible more regularly and spent time in prayer, God would give him the victory he desired.

So he tried. He got out of bed a half hour earlier, read a few verses, and prayed. Nothing happened. Nothing, that is, except that he felt more exhausted during the day. If only he knew for certain that he was forgiven. If only he could have "whatever it takes" to live in fellowship with God.

I am convinced that the greatest single cause of spiritual defeat is a guilty conscience. We know we have sinned and are weary of it; yet we don't know how to be free from a sense of failure. In fact, most of us have experienced the same futile cycle. We sin, we feel guilty, we try to confess our sins, and still our past fills our minds. We then try to do something good to offset our guilt; but the harder we try the more useless it becomes. The result? Discouragement and the suspicion that we have blown it. So we commit the same sins again.

C. S. Lewis, in *Screwtape Letters*, vividly describes Satan's strategy: he gets Christians to become preoccupied with their failures; from then on, the battle is won.

One minister, who has spent many hours counseling people with psychological and spiritual problems, believes that demons are often directly responsible for discouragement and a sense of failure. He has rebuked the demons, and, in many instances, depression has vanished. The caption on the desk of one Christian worker is accurate. It reads: "Discouragement is of the devil."

The greatest blunder of Christians is not their failure

when trying to live for Christ; a greater mistake is that they do not understand God's provision for sin, defeat, and guilt. We are successful to the extent that we understand God's remedy for failure! Read the next few pages carefully: they are an attempt to explain God's cure for the guilt syndrome.

First, Christ's death on the cross included a sacrifice for *all* our sins—past, present, and future. Every sin that you will ever commit has already been paid for. All of our sins were future when Christ died two thousand years ago. Therefore, He made one payment for *all* sins past and future. There is no sin that you will ever commit that has not *already* been included in Christ's death (Colossians 2:13).

God does not find it difficult to forgive us. It is not as though He must regretfully give us a second chance. The price of forgiveness has already been paid, and God wants us to accept it freely.

Christ "is the propitiation for our sins, and not for ours only but also for the sins of the whole world" (1 John 2:2). That means He satisfied God for all sins that can *possibly be committed.* Let me repeat, God has been propitiated (satisfied) for any imaginable evil you might commit.

An atheist asked Billy Graham, "If Hitler had received Christ on his deathbed, would he have gone to heaven, whereas someone who lived a good life but rejected Christ would go to hell?" That is a trick question. It was asked in such a way as to make the gospel appear ridiculous. But the answer is yes. If Hitler accepted Christ, God could forgive him completely, because Christ's death included all of Hitler's sins! God values Christ so much that He can accept Hitler with Christ's merit. Visualize the worst sin imaginable—possibly it is nailing Christ to the cross—Christ died for *that* sin, too.

When Christ cried, "It is finished," the expression is but

one word in Greek, *tetelestai,* a word used for business trans-
actions. When this word was written across a bill, it meant
"paid in full." You need never try to "make up" for your sins
on your own. Christ's death paid for our sins *in full.*

Second, God cannot punish us for our sins. All of the
punishment for sin has already been given to Christ. As Isaiah
predicted, "It was the will of the LORD to crush [Christ]; he
has put him to grief; when his soul makes an offering for
guilt, he shall see his offspring; he shall prolong his days; the
will of the LORD shall prosper in his hand" (Isaiah 53:10).
God bruised Christ; Christ received God's anger for sin. As
William Cowper put it,

> *Death and the curse were in our cup*
> *O Christ, 'twas full for Thee,*
> *But Thou hast drained the last dark drop—*
> *'Tis empty now for me!*
> *Jehovah bade His sword awake,*
> *O, Christ, it woke 'gainst Thee,*
> *Thy blood the flaming blade must slake,*
> *Thy heart its sheath must be*
> *All for my sake—my peace to make,*
> *Now sleeps that sword for me.*

God disciplines us, but He does not punish us. He can
never be angry with us anymore: His justice was satisfied at
the cross. Some Christians interpret all calamities as God
trying to get even with them. A sick child, an accident,
financial problems, all of these are sometimes falsely believed
to be God punishing us for sins.

In fact, some people try to punish *themselves* for their
sins. They often brood over their mistakes and even injure

themselves physically to try to satisfy God. All such attempts to pay for our sin are diabolical. Satan does not want us to understand that Christ paid it all!

Many years ago, a father and his daughter were walking through the grass on the Canadian prairie. In the distance, they saw a prairie fire; eventually, they realized, it would engulf them. The father knew there was only one way of escape: they would quickly build a fire and burn a huge patch of grass. When the huge fire drew near, they then would stand on the section that had already burned. When the fire actually did approach them, the girl was terrified by the raging flames. But her father assured her, "The flames can't get to us. We are standing *where the fire has already been.*"

Are you afraid of God's judgment? If you have trusted Christ as Savior, you can never come under His wrath. When we depend on Him, we are secure; we are where the wrath of God already has been.

Third, although we may become weary of confessing the same sins, God does not become weary of hearing our confession. If we say to God, "I am coming to confess the same sin," God's reply is, "What sin?" Any previous sins that have been confessed *have already been blotted out* forever! "I have blotted out your transgressions like a cloud," God told His people (Isaiah 44:22). David reminds us, "As far as the east is from the west, so far does he remove our transgressions from us" (Psalm 103:12).

When God forgives us, our sins are blotted out so completely that He does not "remember" them (i.e., He never holds them against us again). The sins you confessed yesterday will never again be a barrier between you and God, unless you refuse to accept God's forgiveness and doubt the value of Christ's sacrifice.

Think of a calculator. What happens if you get your information confused or make an error? You can press the "cancel" button. Automatically, all of the information is eliminated from the device. You can begin your calculation again without trying to sort out previous mistakes. In fact, there is no record of the previous information; it is lost forever! That's what happens to our sins when God forgives us. The *consequences* often remain, but the guilt (the legal condemnation for the offense) is gone. If we have a clear conscience toward others (which is brought about by personal confession) we can always have a clear conscience before God.

One of Satan's most popular deceptions is to make us believe that we should not confess our sins until some future time when we are living more "victoriously." Since Satan deceives by feelings as well as words, he gets us to "feel" we are unforgiven; he makes us believe that God is not pleased with our performance, and therefore, we should stop bothering Him about forgiveness!

In order to defend themselves against this attack, Christians often resort to trying to find some sign that God is not displeased with them. They think, "I've received such a blessing from reading my Bible today, surely God must be pleased with me." Or perhaps they have been extra kind or patient. On this basis, they hope to meet Satan's attack. They hope to please God by being victorious, thinking that should give them a more meaningful relationship with the Almighty.

The result? Endless despair and more failure. We are never made acceptable to God by our faithful reading of Scripture or by disciplined prayer (though both are needed). We don't receive God's approval because we witness to others or are faithful at church. God does not even accept us because we do works that He gives us the ability to do! As we shall see later, God is pleased with the good works of His children because of what they signify—love and gratefulness. But the works per se are not the basis of our acceptance.

Our basis for pleasing God? It is standing by faith on the sacrifice of Christ, a sacrifice that satisfied the Father completely. We are accepted *in the beloved.* And that basis remains secure even when we fail!

AN OLD TESTAMENT ILLUSTRATION

When the Israelites were in Egypt, God instructed them to sprinkle blood on the doorpost of their houses. The angel of Jehovah was to pass by the homes that night and kill all the firstborn in Egypt. The only exception would be those homes where blood had been applied. The blood would be for a "sign" upon the houses, and, when the angel saw the blood, he would bypass that particular home.

Let's use our imagination. What if one family decided to hang a list of its achievements on the door of the house? After all, wouldn't God be pleased with their kindness, prayerfulness, and generosity? The answer is obvious. They would have been victims of the plague. God said, "When I see the *blood,* I will pass over you" (Exodus 12:13, emphasis added).

Another family, in their desire to be accepted by God, may have tacked another list of accomplishments to their door. These works were done in genuine devotion to Jehovah and included faithful prayer and separation from sin and sinners. Would that have met God's requirements? Again, no! Only *blood* could please God.

Similarly, Christians have prayed, read the Scriptures, and increased their giving in order to overcome their guilt completely. Their conscience (activated by Satan) tells them that they are failures and that God is not pleased with them. They try to make these accusations by appealing to some of their accomplishments. They hang all of their spiritual victories on the door of their lives, hoping that God will accept them. Satan is delighted! He knows they are hopelessly entangled in one certain failure after another. If they continue, they will end in despair.

Do you want to please God? Do you want His complete acceptance despite your personal failures? You can have that assurance by depending *solely* on Christ's sacrifice.

The purpose of reading the Scriptures and praying is so that our concept of God's salvation will be enlarged and so that we will understand more fully God's gracious (free) provision for all sin. In other words, all those necessary matters we have heard about—devotions, witnessing, prayer—have no *intrinsic* value in God's sight. Only in the beloved Son is God well pleased. And our lives on earth please God only to the extent that our prayers, Bible study, and Christian fellowship increase our appreciation (and application) of God's grace. Then we will voluntarily give ourselves to God in appreciation for what God has given us (Romans 12:1–2; Ephesians 2:8–10).

The implications of this are staggering. Every Christian is equally accepted by God; we all have equal access to fellowship with God.

HOW RIGHTEOUS ARE WE?

How righteous do you have to be in order to get to heaven? The answer is simple: as righteous as God. Of course we all come short of that. But God's standards don't change.

Fortunately, God has a plan to make us that righteous. It

involves forgiving our sins but also much more. A Christian is one who is forgiven *and* has the righteousness of Christ credited to him. God accepts us like He accepts Christ.

Now, since any of us could die at any moment, God has already accepted us *forever* in Christ! That is, *legally*, all of our sins have already been forgiven; Christ's righteousness is ours.

Think of this: God sees believers as absolutely perfect. God sees us in Christ. And *nothing* you can do can change God's complete acceptance of you! Many Christians don't believe this. We are so accustomed to accepting people because of what they are and rejecting them for what they are not, that we believe God must operate like that, too. But if we take God at His word, we must believe that *nothing* we do can stop God from accepting us.

If we are permanently accepted by God, why is it necessary to confess our sins? Our sins block our fellowship, though not our acceptance, with God. To confess means to "agree with God" about our sin. It does not mean to beg, plead, or live in misery until we convince God we mean business. We simply agree that we have sinned and *freely* accept God's forgiveness. When we do this, God does not compromise His justice. "He is faithful and just to forgive us our sins and to cleanse us from all unrighteousness" (1 John 1:9).

The parable of the prodigal son illustrates this point. The wayward son had all of the legal rights of sonship; he had the father's continual acceptance, but he did not enjoy these privileges until he returned to his father and admitted his sins. Similarly, as believers, our acceptance with God is always secure; we have all the rights of sonship, but we must confess our sins to experience the inheritance that is ours.

THE DIFFERENCES BETWEEN CHRISTIANS

Earlier in this book, we showed that the differences between unsaved people were only slight. If we judge Christians by their sins and private failures, the differences between them are not great either; all of us commit sins in our hearts. Why then are some Christians living joyfully and victoriously whereas others live in defeat?

The reason cannot be that some people are more "worthy" in the sight of God than others. Sometimes when we are in special need we ask for the prayers of outstanding Christians. But they do not have special access to God. Blood is blood, whether applied to your doorpost or mine. Christ's sacrifice is no better for one Christian than another! God accepts us on the same basis as the "greats" of the past.

Neither is it because some Christians are not prone to failure; all of us are. In fact, I've concluded that no Christian is an unqualified success. We all experience varying degrees of failure! The difference is in what we do with our mistakes and sins.

Some Christians understand clearly the basis of their acceptance and others don't. Some are not discouraged over failures, because they know that all sins have already been cared for in Christ. Others become preoccupied with their failures and try to find some righteousness *within themselves* to make them worthy to have fellowship with God. *That* is a key difference.

Are you discouraged? Defeated? All of us have been! Micah (a prophet of God, no less) also felt the sting of defeat. But he knew that it need not be permanent. "Rejoice not over me, O my enemy; when I fall, I shall rise; when I sit in darkness, the LORD will be a light to me" (Micah 7:8). Here is a comment from a book of wisdom, "For the righteous falls seven times and rises again, but the wicked stumble in times of calamity" (Proverbs 24:16). Your defeats have been paid for. Say "Thank You" to God and live in fellowship with the Almighty.

FORGIVING OURSELVES

God is not angry with you! He is not displeased with you, if you depend solely on the death and life of Christ for your acceptance.

But one difficulty remains. God is pleased with Christ's sacrifice. He has forgiven you, but *have you forgiven yourself?*

Many Christians are handcuffed by regret. This goes all the way from the widow who says, "If only I had persuaded my husband to go to the doctor earlier, he would not have died," to the person who believes that he has committed the unpardonable sin. By nature, we know that sin has to be paid for; consequently, some people nurse their regrets and cling to their grief. The reason? They believe that such an attitude is necessary to punish themselves. Unconsciously *they* want to pay for their sins.

For example, I know a widow who went to the grave of her husband every morning for fourteen years. Before his death, she had urged him to attend a special event with her. En route, an accident occurred, and later he died. God forgave her mistake (it was not a sin), but she never forgave herself. She felt that if she were ever happy again, it would mean both disrespect for her husband and an indication that she was not truly repentant.

If Christ has paid the penalty for our sins and failures, why should we try to add our continual regret to His work?

Christ came to free us from the bondage of our sin toward God and from our slavery to past failures.

A well-known Christian was driving faster in the rain than was safe. As a result, he was in an accident, and his companion was killed. Regret? Of course! Deep anguish and remorse. Yet, that night, he relates that he saw more clearly than ever before. "The purpose of the cross was to repair the irreparable."

It is the deep, difficult heartaches that the cross was meant to cover. Christ's sacrifice is as good for big sins as it is for small ones. From God's perspective, there is no reason we must be defeated. We are always accepted in God's book, and if our fellowship is broken, it can be restored immediately.

John Newton had committed every sin imaginable. Yet later he understood the reason he could be totally righteous before God. He wrote,

> *Amazing Grace, how sweet the sound*
> *That saved a wretch like me;*
>
> *I once was lost, but now am found.*
> *Was blind but now I see.*

That grace is available for you and me. It is an insult to Christ if we believe His sacrifice was not enough for us!

CHAPTER 6

DO WE GET BY SCOT-FREE?

I'm pregnant. My parents don't know it yet, neither does my boyfriend. I've got to tell somebody. Somebody has to tell me what to do." The speaker was a sixteen-year-old girl brought up in an evangelical church. She was a Christian—a nice Sunday-school kid—the last one you'd expect to see in this condition.

So what do you do? Tell her it's her own fault and that she is getting what she deserves? Hardly. It *is* her own fault; she might be getting what she deserves; but it's too late to sermonize. The girl needs help.

What about God? Should you tell her that she should ask

forgiveness, or would that be making it too easy for someone who should "get what she deserves"? Perhaps God should be brought into the picture only after she has suffered enough, after she has faced embarrassment at the hands of her family and friends?

Of course, this girl needs more than forgiveness. She needs acceptance, understanding, and wisdom. There will be embarrassment, humiliation, and (in certain related cases) church discipline. But so far as her relationship to God is concerned, so far as her *guilt* is concerned, do you encourage her to ask God's forgiveness, or should she come to God after she has gotten other matters straightened out?

It is odd that we should sometimes be tempted to begrudge someone the grace of God at the moment they need it the most. Often we self-righteously believe it unfair that those who sin so grossly should be forgiven so freely.

But forgiveness is already available for every sin that we will ever commit. There is no reason to delay her acceptance of God's grace. Right now, while she is sitting on a chair in your living room, she can be forgiven. Legally (in God's books), her sins that are scarlet can be cleansed like the freshly driven snow. After all, Christ did not come to call the righteous but *sinners* to repentance.

Too simple? Perhaps someone objects, "But if we tell people (especially young people) that forgiveness is readily available, they will live in deliberate sin, knowing they can always count on instant forgiveness." Such a response is wrong but encouraging! When someone says that God's unlimited forgiveness gives license to sin, it shows that they are beginning to understand the incredible generosity of God's grace!

When Paul argued that through Christ we can be forgiven for all our trespasses he stated, "But where sin increased, grace abounded all the more" (Romans 5:20). He knew that if the people understood him correctly—if he made his point clear—his readers would object by in effect saying, "Let us continue in sin that grace might increase!" (Romans 6:1). In other words, once we have grasped the unlimited favor God gives to us, the human (perhaps a better word is *carnal*) reaction is to assume that such teaching will encourage people to sin. Paul's answer is direct: "By no means! How can we who died to sin still live in it?" (Romans 6:2).

Yes, forgiveness is always available to those who repent. God is merciful beyond all human explanation. We can never sin too many times or too much for God to pardon us. We often think that God is like we are. We can forgive the same person a few times, but after that, we have had enough. But God doesn't impose limits on forgiveness. The blood of Christ is never inadequate. It can cover all sins.

Does God's grace encourage sin? Possibly there have been those who have deliberately sinned, flippantly presuming on God's goodness to forgive them. (I think if we were honest, all of us would admit that we have been guilty of that at some time.) But if we do not understand or fully appreciate God's grace, there is a much greater danger: the certainty of discouragement. Because we have been unwilling to explain grace in its fullest sense, many Christians simply do not come to God anymore. They are weary of sin and falsely assume God is weary of them, too.

Only those who understand God's unlimited forgiveness have the wisdom to confess their sins after personal failure. In my counseling, I've learned that most spiritual defeats result from ignorance. Many believers are in the dark as to how good God is and how completely Christ satisfied His requirements for all sin.

Easy believism? Yes! Thank God that the only require-ment for forgiveness is to believe in Him whom He hath sent! To add to that any work or to insist that we must plead and beg for forgiveness is to mix faith and works and insult the Christ who died to save us.

Yes, forgiveness is always free. But that doesn't mean that confession is always easy. Sometimes it is hard. Incredibly hard. It is painful (sometimes literally) to admit our sins and entrust ourselves to God's care.

Think of those who sit in a church pew, convicted of covetousness, pride, and hypocrisy. Forgiveness is free, but admitting to those sins, making restitution, humbling ourselves, these matters are incredibly difficult—so difficult that many Christians would rather be carnal than thoroughly purged. As a result, they prefer simply to confess their sins generally. They want just enough pardon to remain on speaking terms with God, but the core of their lives remains untouched.

Here is the paradox: although forgiveness is free, few people want to receive it. By nature we don't want to admit our sins. If we do, we feel more comfortable in confessing our sins to God than in asking forgiveness of our friends (if we have wronged them). By nature, we don't mind religion, but we resist humility. A broken and contrite heart is not easy to come by.

This is why we often hear that the price of revival (discipleship) is incredibly high. It's not that God's grace costs us anything; it's just that we have to make so many changes when we accept grace in its fullest sense!

Can an unmarried, sixteen-year-old girl who is pregnant receive God's forgiveness freely? Yes. However, whether she will want that forgiveness, whether she will want to face the implications of admitting her sin to God and casting herself upon God's mercy is quite another matter. Remember, confession means that we face our sins head-on. Most of us prefer to dodge our sins, work them out ourselves, or, if possible, ignore them. Jeremiah says the heart is deceitful above all things. Little wonder we are experts at deceiving others and ourselves.

This unmarried girl can be forgiven, but the requirement is that she agree with God that *she* has sinned. As long as it's the boyfriend's fault, the parents' fault, or the church's fault, she cannot have fellowship with God.

There is also another lesson in this story: forgiveness wipes out guilt before God and restores us to fellowship. But forgiveness cannot eliminate the consequences of sin. Some sins have especially serious effects that can never be erased in this life. Let's consider this in more detail.

THE SOCIAL CONSEQUENCES

All sins have consequences. Even the sins of the mind are not as harmless as we often suppose. True, there are sometimes no visible effects of sinful thoughts. Although all sins are conceived in the mind, they need not give birth to actions. But even so, evil thoughts weaken our moral and spiritual resistance to temptation. If we lust we will not necessarily commit the act of adultery, but the lust prepares the way for the overt act. Furthermore, there are some sins—great sins— that often exist solely in the mind. Pride and covetousness are examples.

Although we might not always (or ever) see the result of our thoughts, God judges us by them just the same. "As [a man] thinks within himself, so he is" (Proverbs 23:7 NASB).

Christ severely rebuked the Pharisees who cleaned the outside of the cup but inside were full of robbery and self-indulgence (Matthew 23:25). He told them that they should clean their hearts first and then be concerned about outward conduct.

Yet, it is our actions that have the most far-reaching consequences. The pregnant sixteen-year-old could be forgiven, but the child would be born. The murderer who receives forgiveness is clothed in Christ's righteousness but must still serve his prison sentence. The carnal Christian who receives forgiveness for specific sins (and makes personal adjustments) can walk with God, but there is no way to restore the lost time.

Possibly, the most familiar biblical illustration of sin's consequences is David's story. In a moment of passion he committed adultery with Bathsheba. His story is unique because he was not an uncommitted, flippant man whose life was characterized by wickedness. He was chosen to be king precisely because he was "a man after God's own heart." David's experience reminds us that *none* of us is beyond the possibility of gross sin. Greater men than we have thrown away their purity in a moment of sensual passion. The one who believes he stands (i.e., the one who believes he or she could never do such a thing) is the most likely to fall.

David's experience also illustrates how difficult it is to ask for forgiveness. Undoubtedly, his conscience troubled him, but he did not want to face the painful consequences of confession. His guilt was so pronounced that it even affected his physical condition: "For when I kept silent, my bones wasted away through my groaning all day long. For day and night your hand was heavy upon me; my strength was dried up as by the heat of summer" (Psalm 32:3–4). Yet, for all that, David did not repent of his sin.

Even when Nathan the prophet told the parable to illustrate David's sin, the king did not get the message. Finally, the prophet confronted David directly. Then David repented.

Did God forgive him? Yes. Even in the Old Testament era the repentant were forgiven. But the consequences were disastrous; God predicted that there would be fighting within David's family; his wives would be raped in broad daylight, and Bathsheba's son would die. In the end, David also lost his sons Absalom and Ammon.

Stiff consequences? Yes. But some sins—particularly sexual ones—have bitter repercussions. In Scripture, sexual immorality is especially singled out as one sin that is most harmful (1 Corinthians 6:17–20). Those who give their body to another in an illicit relationship (whether it is public knowledge or not) bear special emotional and moral scars.

Sometimes Christians, in order to dramatize God's complete forgiveness, say, "The bird with the broken wing will fly just as high again," implying that any sinner can be restored to his original usefulness if he truly repents.

I disagree. The story of David, plus a host of similar illustrations in contemporary life, proves that the bird with the broken wing often does *not* fly as high as he did before. Sometimes he never flies again! There are some consequences for specific sins that we will carry to our grave.

However, as emphasized earlier in this book, all is never lost. God does make the best of our consequences; He does use our self-inflicted problems for ultimate good. To return once more to the story of David, it was after he finally did confess his sins that he had the assurance of God's guidance again. The same psalm that speaks of how painful confession is also tells how satisfying God's leading is. God reminds David, "I will instruct you and teach you in the way you should go;

I will counsel you with my eye upon you. . . . Be glad in the LORD, and rejoice, O righteous, and shout for joy, all you upright in heart!" (Psalm 32:8, 11). When God forgives, He gives us the ability to rejoice, even in the middle of tragedies that are our own fault. The greatest sinner can yet give praise to God. The consequences might remain; the guilt does not.

GOD'S DISCIPLINE

God does not punish Christians for sin. God disciplines His children, but He doesn't punish them. The distinction is this: punishment carries the idea of satisfying justice for a crime. But Christ satisfied the Father's justice. Therefore, God now disciplines us, that is, He brings problems and struggles into our lives so that we will not stray from the main road. He is not angry with us but disciplines us so that we can mature spiritually.

Of course God doesn't scold us or make us stand in the corner. But He does use the circumstances of life to keep us in line. In fact, He scourges (whips) every son that belongs to Him (Hebrews 12:6).

Those to whom the book of Hebrews was written were tempted to become discouraged because of persecution. They hadn't yet had to die for their faith, but they were on the verge of buckling under pressure.

These problems did not come to them because they were unlucky. Their circumstances were God's way of developing their faith and weaning them from the attractions of the world. God was disciplining them for their own good so that they might be partakers of His holiness (Hebrews 12:10). God disciplines *all* of his children (Hebrews 12:8), and if someone is not corrected by Him, he is an illegitimate child.

The upshot of this is that we should learn everything we can from the difficulties of life without complaining about the way our Father treats us.

Should we interpret all of our problems as the result of specific sins? The obvious answer is no. Those whose lives are filled with tragedy are not necessarily more sinful than those who are free from such difficulties. But in each instance we can be certain of one fact: God intends to teach us faith and conform us to Christ. As a result, He will not screen us from anything that will help us reach these goals.

Of course we do sometimes encounter difficulties as a direct result of specific sins. We've already emphasized that sins—especially *some* sins—have damaging consequences. But in many instances we may not know whether our tragedies are the direct result of specific sins. Often calamities hit us without any apparent connection between our actions and a given sin.

The point is this: *it isn't necessary to know why God sent us the misfortune in order to profit from it.* Just because we can't think of any specific reason for the trial doesn't mean that God had no reason for allowing it.

We can be sure that God's primary concern for us is always that we forsake our sins and develop the rich qualities of faith and joy *within* our circumstances. The writer of Hebrews observed that discipline is usually not welcomed, "but later it yields the peaceful fruit of righteousness to those who have been trained by it" (12:11).

All of our difficulties—whether the result of our own sin or not—are custom-designed by God to teach us how to apply His grace. Even Paul had to learn that God's grace was sufficient for his thorn in the flesh.

Paul said he had *learned* to be content in every circumstance of life (Philippians 4:11). The implication is that contentment is not a quality that comes naturally. If Paul had to learn from poverty, shipwrecks, hunger, and imprisonment, perhaps we need a few roadblocks in our lives to learn the same lesson.

Tragically, many Christians who complain about life are not learning the lessons God wants to teach them. They are like a child who simply resents his parents' spankings and refuses to profit from them. Yet, the irony is that God often simply applies more pressure when we are too stubborn to get the message!

When some ships are brought into the harbor, they must be steered through the deepest section of the harbor or else be broken on the rocks. Similarly, some Christians have been spared personal shipwreck (even though they might not know it) when they have come through the deepest waters of misfortune.

Remember, God always disciplines in love. God cannot be angry with us, neither can He ever punish us since Christ received punishment for us. All of the ammunition of God's justice was exhausted for *our good*, that is, to lead us to more meaningful relationships with God.

Confession removes all guilt but not necessarily all consequences. God uses these circumstances (and the dilemmas of life in general) to develop rich qualities (the fruit of the Spirit) within us. Therefore, we can experience a joyful relationship with God, even when facing problems that are our own fault.

CHAPTER 7

A FOUNDATION FOR SELF-ACCEPTANCE

Mary looked as if she'd never had a problem in her life. She was friendly, attractive, and cheerful. But beneath that facade were feelings too deep for words—feelings of resentment, bitterness, and intolerable depression. In fact, she had contemplated suicide.

That she was a dedicated Christian made her problem more puzzling. Why did Christ not give her the fulfillment she craved? Why was she beset with uncontrollable resentment? She had spent countless hours in prayer asking God for deliverance, but to no avail. Although Christ came to set His people free, this woman was in bondage.

Mary's background provided the clue to her problem. Her father died when she was a child, and, as a result, she was entrusted to the care of a harsh stepfather who vented his bitterness on this unwanted child. When Mary (then three or four years old) would come to her stepfather for affection, she was brushed aside. One remark he made will always ring in her ears: "I'd like to throw you out! You should be pushed into a ditch."

Understandably, Mary grew up feeling guilty for simply being alive. She felt responsible for her stepfather's misery and developed deep feelings of inferiority. She knew that she would always be a failure. Furthermore, she believed she *deserved* to be one.

In later years, when friends showed concern for her, she resented it. *How could anyone ever love me?* she thought. She believed no person in his right mind would love someone as worthless as she. She even married a man whom she believed did not love her. *No sane, decent, respectable man would love me,* she unconsciously assumed. Thus, she settled for something less than love (at least from her perspective) when she promised to "love, honor, and obey."

Twenty years and four children later, she began verbalizing her true feelings. At first I believed she was looking for sympathy, fishing for compliments. But I was mistaken. This beautiful and intelligent woman believed she was the scum of the earth; she believed with all her heart, mind, and soul that she was and always would be a colossal failure, a gigantic zero.

Mary's self-image could not be changed merely by telling her that her opinion of herself was mistaken. Those who reject themselves cannot be convinced to accept themselves by pointing out their personal worth or accentuating their positive qualities. The point is they *feel* inferior, they *feel* worthless, they *feel* rejected. No amount of persuasion can convince them otherwise.

Consequently, beautiful people may actually believe they are ugly; talented people may believe they are inferior; and people who are loved may reject the love they so desperately crave.

Even those who have grown up in fine homes—Christian homes—often find difficulty with self-acceptance. A person who flunks college, fails on a business venture, or is fired from a job may find that it takes years for him to accept his failure. He may never regain the self-confidence he once had. But God has not left us without hope.

Fortunately, it is possible to accept ourselves even after we have failed. Even if we were rejected by our parents, friends, or marriage partner we can accept ourselves—failure and all. But we can only do this by facing our limitations and considering our lot in life from God's perspective.

When I speak of accepting our failures I don't mean that we should accept habitual sin as a way of life. Rather, I am suggesting that God wants us to put past failures behind us and not use them as an excuse for morbid introspection, pessimism, or depression. Self-acceptance means that we are at peace with ourselves, with others, and with God.

People reject themselves for many reasons: physical appearance, lack of ability and intelligence, or because of the failures of the past. Others, like Mary, have warped views of themselves because of their family background. Thank God this can be changed! The Scriptures provide the information necessary to be at peace with ourselves and be free from the bondage of self-rejection.

ACCEPTING OUR LIMITATIONS

Our opinion of ourselves is formed largely by the attitude of others toward us. If, as children, we are ridiculed for our physical appearance or our lack of ability, we may develop deep-seated inferiority and the belief that we are doomed to be a failure.

Children are often unintentionally cruel in pointing out one another's physical idiosyncrasies. If a child is too fat, too skinny, too tall, or too short, he can become so self-conscious that he loses his self-respect and self-esteem. Sometimes the emotional scars are so deep that the person may never develop self-confidence again.

In fact, most people who reject themselves do so because they dislike their physical appearance. They look in the mirror and wonder where God was when they were put together. As a result they feel self-conscious, worthless, and inferior. They may unconsciously or consciously hate God because of the way He made them.

What do the Scriptures teach regarding our physical appearance? First, God fashioned us in our mother's womb (Psalm 139:13–16). Therefore, our appearance was determined by Him. In fact, God even takes responsibility for physical handicaps. To Moses he said, "Who has made man's mouth? Who makes him mute, or deaf, or seeing, or blind? Is it not I, the LORD?" (Exodus 4:11). God made us the way we are for a special reason. We must accept the fact that He knew what He was doing when we were assembled. We will never accept our physical features unless we thank God that He made us as He did.

Of course there may be some things about ourselves that we can change; our weight, for instance. If we are overweight we should diet, and all of us should take care of ourselves physically and work to improve our abilities. But God takes responsibility for the basic "raw material" we have to work with.

The first step? Thank God for the way He made you. *You* are special, distinct, and unique. You were not made from a common mold. Thank Him that you are special.

Second, we must see that God created us less than ideal (i.e., with our physical or functional handicaps) to teach us that the inward is more important than the outward. Rich qualities of character make a truly beautiful person. A Korean minister who had been the pastor of a large congregation of lepers made this observation: "Despite their leprosy, they were beautiful people *inside.*"

Inside! Isn't that what God said to Samuel when he was trying to find a king for Israel? Samuel thought that one of the tall, impressive sons of Jesse would qualify. But God had other ideas. He explained to Samuel, "Do not look on his appearance or on the height of his stature, because I have rejected him. For the LORD sees not as man sees: man looks on the outward appearance, but the LORD looks on the heart" (1 Samuel 16:7). It's the *inside* that counts.

Peter taught the same truth in the New Testament. Since women (and men) are often conscious—perhaps too conscious—of their appearance, Peter taught that the emphasis should not be on the outward adorning: "But let your adorning be the hidden person of the heart with the imperishable beauty of a gentle and quiet spirit, which in God's sight is very precious" (1 Peter 3:4). Our outward imperfections are a reminder of God's priorities. He is concerned with character, not the deception of outward beauty.

On the surface it would seem that those who are especially good-looking have an advantage over the rest of us, and, to some extent, this is true. We are taught to worship the god of beauty early in life. Attractive children, teenagers, and adults are usually the most popular and the most accepted. Yet, inherent in such advantages are many dangers. Those who are physically attractive find it much more difficult to accept the onslaught of old age, and, even more important, they face greater temptations. The attractive are often lured into promiscuity and frequently sense they are loved for how they look rather than for what they are.

If we are dissatisfied with our appearance, God is trying to teach us to find our security *in Him.* He knows that if we were attractive we might find our satisfaction in the fleeting pleasure of popularity rather than the solid rock of inward godliness.

Others resent God because of their lack of intelligence or lack of ability. They spend their lives wishing they were like someone else; their conversation is filled with self-pity and self-derogatory comments. Perhaps they believe that such an attitude displays humility. They never seem to grow weary of informing others of their shortcomings.

Such an attitude is not humility; neither is it realism; it is sin. And there will be no victory over such an ungrateful attitude until it is confessed and forsaken.

God has given us our abilities. If we are gifted, we cannot take credit for it; if we lack abilities, that is no reason to complain. To the Corinthians, who prided themselves in their spiritual gifts, Paul wrote, "For who sees anything different in you? What do you have that you did not receive? If then you received it, why do you boast as if you did not receive it?" (1 Corinthians 4:7). One of our temptations is to overestimate the importance of our abilities. Often we build up such an unrealistic self-image that we cannot—or, perhaps, will not—face our limitations. Or we may go to the other extreme and underestimate our gifts.

The solution? Take Paul's advice: "I say to everyone among you not to think of himself more highly than he ought to think, but to think with sober judgment, each according to the measure of faith that God has assigned" (Romans 12:3). We must evaluate our abilities realistically, accept our limitations, and thank God for *whatever* He has given us.

History is filled with innumerable instances of people who refused to be stopped by handicaps, misfortune, and lack of ability. They understood that a lack of personal ability did not cramp God's power; indeed, His strength is made perfect in weakness. They were able to praise God for what He had given them, and, in the process, they accepted themselves for what they were.

Self-acceptance is basically a spiritual issue. What it boils down to is this: Are we able to thank the Creator for the way He made us? If not, we are casting doubt on His wisdom; if we can thank Him, we display our belief that He knows what is best for us. And *that* will help us accept ourselves— limitations, failures, and all.

But even more than this, we must come to appreciate our value from God's perspective. Understanding His acceptance of us gives us the key to understanding ourselves.

THEOLOGICAL CONSIDERATION

Theologians have often erred by not distinguishing between proper self-love (i.e., self-acceptance) and selfishness. It is true that we should not love ourselves in a self-centered way, but it is equally true that we must not hate ourselves. We must accept ourselves, for if we are not at peace with ourselves, we cannot be at peace with others or with God. The Scriptures teach that we should love our neighbor *as* we do ourselves. We cannot love our neighbor unless we, in a proper sense, love ourselves.

Sometimes we are told, "We are nothing in God's sight. We are worms before Him." In one sense this is true; namely, that we are rebellious sinners who cannot do one iota to please God on our own. But in another more profound sense, such a statement is patently false. Would Christ have died for us if we were worthless? Would He (pardon the thought) have died for worms?

The scriptural viewpoint is that all people are exceedingly valuable in God's sight, so valuable that God gave the best He had to redeem us. His investment in us is so great He could not possibly abandon us.

An illustration might help. Let us imagine a husband who invests his life's savings to buy a diamond for his wife. Would he be careless with it? Or would he treasure and protect it with painstaking care? The answer is obvious: since the diamond was purchased at a high cost, it will be protected, polished, and admired. Its value lies in its cost.

We were not bought with money but with the precious blood of Christ. If the value of an item depends on the price paid for it, the worth of each believer (and unbeliever, too, since Christ died for the whole world) is beyond calculation. Since God's investment in us is so great He is not about to abandon us. He is interested in protecting His valuables.

A poet can take a worthless sheet of paper, write a poem on it, and make it worth thousands of dollars. An artist can take a canvas, paint a picture, and the masterpiece becomes more valuable than gold. God takes sinners, redeems them with the sacrifice of His Son, and gives them the Holy Spirit as a pledge of His ownership. Then He elevates them to become joint heirs with Christ, His Son. Yet, some of these believers insist that they are worthless property!

To return to Mary, she began to make progress when she grasped the significance of God's investment in her as an individual. She realized that God is not an unwise speculator. He doesn't make foolish investments. In rejecting herself, Mary was, in effect, telling God that He is an unwise investor. He paid a high price for worthless property. If we feel worthless or hate ourselves, we insult Him.

In a sense, God's honor is at stake in us. David wrote that the Lord leads us in paths of righteousness, not merely for our own good, but for *His name's sake* (Psalm 23:3). Since we are His, He has the responsibility of protecting His investment. His reputation is at stake.

To repeat, regardless of how worthless we might feel, God thinks differently. Anyone—and particularly believers—can say, "I am valuable to God." To say less than that is to cast doubt on God's reputation. He knew what He was doing when He bought us at a high cost.

ACCEPTING IN THE BELOVED

If you were a first-century slave who ran away from your owner, what would you expect as punishment when you returned? A flogging? Death?

That's what the slave Onesimus might have expected. But fortunately the apostle Paul intervened on his behalf. This incident illustrates what God has done for us.

Onesimus would probably have been glad simply to be forgiven. He'd have been glad if the past were forgotten and if he could begin again. Forgiveness brings great relief.

Many people believe that a Christian is simply a sinner whose sins are forgiven. They are grateful that God gives them a fresh start, and, as far as they are concerned, that is all they need. Yet, after repeatedly confessing the same sin, they become discouraged. Then they begin to wonder whether God's patience is wearing thin; perhaps He is not accepting them anymore.

Forgiveness is a precious gift! But forgiveness alone does not give us the security we need to live the Christian life. The forgiveness of specific sins does not guarantee our continual acceptance before God.

When Paul wrote a letter to Philemon on behalf of Onesimus, he requested more than forgiveness. He asked Philemon to accept Onesimus as he would accept the apostle himself. He wrote, "*If* you consider me your partner, receive him as you would receive me" (Philemon 17, emphasis added). Onesimus was not to be merely a forgiven slave; he was to be received and treated *as if* he were the apostle Paul.

Let me say it once more. If your defeats and failures cause you to turn away from God, you don't understand God's grace. Christ died so that we would have the basis of acceptance before God that has *nothing* to do with our fluctuating experiences. Our acceptance depends on the sacrifice of Christ on the cross.

In God's sight there are only two classes of people, those who are in Christ and those who are outside of Him. And all those who are in Christ are accepted equally; there are no grades of perfection with God.

Of course, in actual experience Christians differ: some are carnal, others are godly, and the majority are somewhere in between. But there is no difference so far as *acceptance* is concerned.

We can't question Christ's acceptability to the Father. God the Father said that Christ is His beloved Son in whom He is well pleased. Yet we are just as pleasing to God as Christ! Christ, as it were, says to God the Father, "Receive these believers *as* You receive Me."

This illustrates the mind-boggling New Testament teaching that believers are not merely forgiven; they are not merely sinners minus their sins, but they are accepted before God as Christ is accepted! They are accepted in the Beloved (Ephesians 1:6).

Again, our acceptance before God is based squarely on Christ's acceptance before the Father. There can be no such thing as degrees of acceptance with God. He accepts perfection only for the reason that Christ alone is acceptable to the Father. The good news is that when we receive Christ as Savior, we are accepted *in Him*. Our acceptance before God is as certain as Christ's!

Perhaps you have flown in an airplane. Did the stewardess ask you whether you had a good day before you were permitted to board? Were you rejected if you were depressed?

Of course not. As far as the airline is concerned, you could be depressed, elated, or apathetic. Only one thing qualifies you for the flight: the right ticket. And that ticket has nothing to do with your feelings!

Imagine a man standing in the terminal with his boarding pass in hand, refusing to enter the plane because he feels unworthy to fly! Such an attitude would prove that he doesn't understand the basis for his admittance to the plane. He would probably end up a nervous wreck and never get off the ground. He doesn't understand that his worthiness or unworthiness is not the issue; the *ticket* is what counts.

Think of the implications. If God (whose standards are

far higher than ours) has completely forgiven and accepted us, why can we not accept ourselves? Why can we not believe His verdict in the matter and accept ourselves as He accepts us? If we have received the ticket, which Christ paid for on the cross, we have no need to feel unacceptable.

Perhaps now we can understand why those who reject themselves (and, as a result, experience deep depression) do not find help through prayer. Tim LaHaye, who has had vast experience in counseling, has observed that a high percentage of depressed people frequently pray. But their prayers remain unanswered because (1) they use the occasion to repeat their failures, indulge in self-pity, and remind God of their worthlessness; and (2) their prayer is, of necessity, one of unbelief. They spend most of their time praying that God will accept them, and they refuse to believe His word, namely, the fact that *He already has!*

We need not look within ourselves to find some reason that God should accept us. Neither should we believe that God rejects us because we are unworthy. True, we *are* unworthy, but our acceptance is unrelated to our unworthiness. We are received in Christ; His righteousness is attributed to us.

This is the heart of the doctrine of justification by faith. God declares us righteous. We are credited with all the perfection of Christ!

Have you accepted yourself, failures, limitations, physical handicaps, and all? If your faith is in Christ, *God has accepted you* just as you are. To reject yourself is to reject God's grace.

Accepting ourselves does not mean that we condone sin or that we simply learn to adjust to continual spiritual failures. As explained above, God accepts a Christian who persistently lives in sin, but God is not honored by the life of such a Christian.

Here is the point. Our acceptance before God gives us the security to turn repeatedly to God for strength and forgiveness. *Our acceptance in heaven gives us the basis to live here on earth.* God's legal declaration—that we are credited with the righteousness of Christ—makes it possible for us to be free from guilt, free from the emotional scars of the past.

Mary illustrates the point. When she began to thank God for His acceptance of her through Christ, when she realized how valuable she was to God, her attitude toward herself began to change. At last she was free to live without self-condemnation, free to return to God for spiritual power, free to evaluate honestly her abilities and appearance. Although her stepfather did not accept her, she found comfort in David's words: "For my father and my mother have forsaken me, but the LORD will take me in" (Psalm 27:10).

CHAPTER 8

THE DETOUR
CAN LEAD BACK TO
THE MAIN ROAD

The woman sat quietly, carefully pondering her next sentence. Then she leaned forward in her chair, as if to give special emphasis to each word. "God can't bless us. We can't be happy. *We should never have been married.*"

Her story? She was reared in a Christian home. As she grew older, she deeply resented her parents' restrictions, especially because they disapproved of the boys she dated. The arguments that erupted only drove a deeper wedge between their beliefs and hers. She determined to do as she pleased. And she did.

By the time she announced her wedding, she was

already three months pregnant.

Deep within, she was bitter. She knew her parents had been right in what they had told her, but she was too proud to admit it. She swore her marriage would work.

It didn't.

Her husband was not the carefree and thoughtful man she had believed he was. She felt trapped because she *had* to marry him. He felt the same way about her.

She spent hours dreaming of what she *might* have done, whom she *might* have married, if she had not become attached to this—this thing. It was pride, the determination not to admit they were wrong, that held their marriage together.

Years later, she finally asked God to forgive her sins. Slowly she was able to work through her bitterness, depend on God's mercy, and accept herself for what she was. So far, her husband was unchanged.

And now she found herself wondering about God's will for her life. She wished that God could bless her and her husband. But could she honestly expect God's help in their marriage after her deliberate disobedience?

Maybe she was supposed to have been a missionary. There was little use trying to speculate. The fact remained that she was married to a man whom God never intended for her. How could she be happy now that she was *permanently* ("till death do us part") out of God's will?

What happens when Christians marry the wrong partner, refuse to accept God's call to be a missionary, or bypass countless opportunities because of unbelief? Can they ever again prove that "good and acceptable and perfect will of God"?

Sometimes we get the impression that the will of God is

like an egg, a heavenly Humpty-Dumpty. Presumably, God expects us to do a balancing act as we walk an invisible tightrope. One mistake—or, at the most, two—and no one, not even God, can put Humpty-Dumpty together again.

Of course it is true that one sin (or even an error in judgment) can be costly. One immoral relationship, one selfish choice, or one bypassed opportunity can have devastating consequences. But we must remember that God is never finished with anyone who repents. Anyone can be forgiven; anyone can yet do the will of God.

Let me explain.

GOD'S IDEAL WILL

Does God have an ideal plan for everyone's life? To answer this, let us begin one step further back: Does God have an ideal plan for the world? Presumably, an ideal world was the Garden of Eden; His ideal people were Adam and Eve.

Sin ruined this perfect setup. Disobedience brought evil and death to the human race. Sin even affected the planet, and all of nature was cursed.

Did the Fall of man cause an emergency in heaven? Was God in despair, thinking that mankind could never have fellowship with Him again?

No! God did not have to hurriedly depend on a makeshift backup plan. He was not caught off guard. Christ's coming was not a last-minute decision made in the wake of a disaster. Redemption was planned long before sin entered the world (Titus 1:2).

God, who knows and controls all things, had already planned to take a ruined world and incorporate it into His program. Since Adam sinned, God has been working *in*, *with,* and *in spite of* sinful conditions.

The ideal world was ruined; but God instituted another "ideal" plan, that is, the plan of redemption. God chose to use evil to accomplish His ultimate purpose. Evil is not an enemy that took God by surprise. God has not chosen to destroy evil by one sovereign act. Rather, He has chosen to let it exist and redeem us from it. Where sin abounds, grace *does* much more abound!

To talk about the "ideal" life is quite futile. Since we were all born as children of wrath, we have all experienced sins and failures. The only ideal life will be in heaven, and if you are reading this, you're not there!

Of course, within the context of our sinful human condition, God undoubtedly has a plan for everyone's life. It includes such matters as our vocation, marriage partner (or lack of one), and even minute details of everyday life. The very hairs of our head are numbered. But all such plans are made by taking our sinful condition into account. For God, there are no contingencies; He knows the end from the beginning.

What if we should err on one point or another? What if we disobey God and sin greatly? Or marry the "wrong" one? God will not be caught off guard. He will not be forced to activate emergency equipment. *He is as prepared to help us in our sin as He was to help Adam in his.*

God is a specialist in the sin disease. His Son died to remedy our situation. And if we repent and seek Him, *He will make the best arrangement possible within the context of our failure.*

As a result, we never reach the place where God is no longer willing to direct us. True, we might damage God's plan and pay the consequences. But if we repent, God will make the best of every situation. He is well prepared to work in and through conditions that are less than ideal.

To understand how this works in practice, let's consider four examples.

Example one: I know a man who believed that God wanted him to be a missionary in Europe. He refused to go. Later he yielded himself to God, and now he is an effective witness to others on this continent. He ends each day with the satisfaction of having been guided by God.

God is never short on ideas. He never says, "You blew it! I can't work you in." He does not run a union that can handle only a prescribed quota of workers. We are not permanently unemployed in the kingdom of heaven because we've shown up late for work. Neither are we on a waiting list, knowing that someone else must retire before we are hired. If we are willing to do anything (even things we thought we were not trained for), our God can use us.

Example two: A woman who came to me for counsel has a struggling marriage. As a Christian, she had married a non-Christian. She has paid dearly for that decision.

But now she has finally submitted herself totally to God. As a result, God is blessing her. The rough edges of her character are being smoothed by the struggles of her marriage. Her self-made predicament is teaching her the rich qualities of love, joy, peace, and patience.

Sometimes the going is tough, but God isn't through with her. She has already led her children to Christ.

Example three: Remember Jonah? God said, "Go to Nineveh." Jonah said, "No, I'm going to Tarshish." He ended up in the stomach of a fish. Was he in God's will? In one sense he was not, for he should have been going to Nineveh. But because of his disobedience, God prepared the fish for Jonah. The fish (and its appetite) was arranged under God's directive will. Jonah was disobedient, but God had other plans for His servant. The plan included a scary ride to Nineveh.

Remember, God is concerned that we stay in His will. He went to the trouble of preparing a fish, a storm, and even loaded the sailors' dice so that Jonah would get back on course. If God did this for a prophet who deliberately disobeyed, think of what He will do for those who fully commit their ways to Him.

Example four: Jephthah was an illegitimate child, "the son of a prostitute" (Judges 11:1). After he grew up, he was forced out of his home because of his discredited birth. Later he was asked to return to his relatives and fight the Ammonites.

Does God have a purpose for a man who is the unintended product of an illicit sexual relationship? Can God use someone who, strictly speaking, should never have been born? Yes. "Then the Spirit of the Lord was upon Jephthah.... So Jephthah crossed over to the Ammonites to fight against them, and the Lord gave them into his hand" (Judges 11:29, 32).

Many people have had the crushing experience of being rejected by their parents. Often they develop such a low self-image that they are convinced that no one—including God—could possibly love them. Perhaps they are humiliated by the circumstances of their conception or their debased surroundings.

Here is good news: God can incorporate *any* repentant sinner into His program! When our father and mother forsake us. He will take us up (Psalm 27:10). There is no such thing as a situation beyond God's control.

KNOWING GOD'S WILL

God does not want us to be ignorant of His will. Too often we think of the will of God as mystical or private information that can be known only by those who are "called" into vocational Christian work. Yet, the Scriptures say to us all, "Therefore do not be foolish, but understand what the will of the Lord is" (Ephesians 5:17). God does not play hide-and-seek; He wants us to know His will.

Unfortunately, many Christians are confused at this point. They think of the will of God almost solely in geographical terms: Where shall we live? Or as a vocational decision: What should my occupation be? But all of these decisions are secondary; they fall into place after the most important aspects of God's will have been done.

It sounds trite, but the will of God is spelled out clearly for us in Scripture. God has desires that apply to all Christians. He does not have one will for missionaries and another for bricklayers. True, God may lead them into different vocations, but His primary will for all of us is the same.

What does God want *you* to do? A group of people asked Jesus, "What must we do, to be doing the works of God?" (John 6:28). That is a sensible question. Christ answered, "This is the work of God, that you believe in him whom he has sent" (v. 29). God's first purpose for our lives is that we transfer our trust from ourselves to Christ; that we believe in Him. What does God want *you* to do? First, He wants you personally to trust Christ as your Savior.

Second, God wants you to live in moral purity. "For this is the will of God, your sanctification: that you abstain from sexual immorality. . . . For God has not called us for impurity, but in holiness" (1 Thessalonians 4:3, 7). God wants us to be free from sensuality, both in our actions and in our thoughts.

Many Christians have secret moral sins that have captivated their minds. Some have already given up in the struggle. God wills that we learn to apply Christ's victory to ourselves. *That* is His will for you and me.

What else? "Give thanks in all circumstances; for this is the will of God in Christ Jesus for you" (1 Thessalonians 5:18). An attitude of thankfulness shows our faith in God's providence.

Sometimes Christians say, "I want to glorify God in my life." But what does that mean? How do you glorify God? Who is qualified to glorify the Almighty? Here is the answer: "The one who offers thanksgiving as his sacrifice glorifies me" (Psalm 50:23).

It is also God's will that we do our routine duties with enthusiasm and joy. Listen to what Paul wrote to slaves who were often mistreated and expected to do the most humiliating chores. He urged them to be obedient, and then added that they should serve "with a sincere heart, as you would Christ, not by the way of eye-service, as people-pleasers, but as bondservants of Christ, doing the will of God from the heart" (Ephesians 6:5–6).

What is God's will for a homemaker who dislikes washing dishes and clothes and who lives with an ungrateful husband? It is to do her work with joy, just as if she were doing these things for Christ.

What is God's will for a man who dislikes both his employer and his job? It is to work as though Christ is the one who hands him the paycheck at the end of the week. *That* is the will of God.

There are numerous other commands in Scripture relating to our basic attitudes (Romans 12). But all of these commands, including those referred to above, state specifically what God's will is for us. Yet, remarkably, these commands can be applied to *all* Christians, even those whose lives have a history of failures and sins. Since God is primarily concerned about our attitudes and responses, *anyone* can do the will of God. Even if we have made unwise choices, bypassed opportunities, or sinned miserably, it is not too late to begin to do what God wants us to do!

GOD'S SPECIFIC DIRECTION

But what about other choices that involve God's will, those that are not mentioned in the Bible? Obviously, Scripture cannot tell us whether we should become missionaries to another country or whether we should go to college. Each of us makes a host of such decisions daily. How do we determine God's will in these matters?

The formula is quite simple. If we are obedient in the plan God has revealed, He is obligated to guide us in decisions that are unrevealed. If we houseclean our attitudes, values, and desires, if we seek first the kingdom of God and His righteousness, these other matters will be added unto us.

God has an indefinite number of ways to block us if we are going the wrong way and to create opportunities if we are going the right way. For example, He guides us by the advice of others and the desires He puts within us.

What about Brian and his wife described in chapter 1? They failed as missionaries. Is God finished with them? No. God can use their failure to teach them lessons on faith and acceptance. They can still do the will of God! By accepting their failure and giving God their future, they can be both blessed and a blessing to others.

What about the woman who married an unbeliever?

If she accepts God's forgiveness and seeks His will, she will experience God's guidance. In fact, I've known many Christians in similar circumstances who have done just that. If we are obedient to God's Word, He is faithful to guide us in the mundane experiences of life.

But the hard part is this: we have to confess and forsake our sins. After David sinned with Bathsheba, his fellowship with God was repaired only when he admitted his guilt—with all of its implications. He realized that "the sacrifices of God are a broken spirit; a broken and contrite heart, O God, you will not despise" (Psalm 51:17).

One day some ink was accidentally spilled onto a beautiful and expensive handkerchief. The mess was observed by an artist who decided to make the best of the situation. So he drew a picture on the cloth and used the blotch of ink as part of the scenery. God is well equipped to do that for us, if we are prepared to let Him. The cost? A broken and a contrite heart.

It is never too late to do God's will. Failures of the past sometimes curtail our ministry, but they need not poison our attitude. The past cannot be changed, but our response to it can be. If we acknowledge God in all our ways, He will yet direct our paths!

CHAPTER 9

THERE IS A PRICE

The tragedy made headlines for ten days. Radio and television stations kept replaying the story. As people exchanged greetings in stores and on the street, this event surfaced as the number-one topic of conversation. A murder is always news, but this one made the community stagger in disbelief.

The story? A mother was murdered by her own fifteen-year-old son. The young rebel had killed the one who had borne and nurtured him. The ordeal was even more shocking because the people involved were Christians. The father had studied for the ministry and was a lay preacher. Now he suffered the humiliation of standing beside the casket of his wife, who was the victim of their own flesh and blood.

The man became disillusioned with God and bitter with other believers. He felt justified in his attitude for one good reason: fellow believers, who should have stood with him through this painful experience, rejected him. "Any man with a family like that should never hold office in a church again," they reasoned.

Eight years later, the brokenhearted man suffered a second crushing blow: one of his other sons committed suicide. "For ten years I lived one-half inch from hell," he said. "No one will ever know the darkness I experienced." Like water spilled on the ground, the past could not be reclaimed. There was only the future, and that looked as black as the darkness of the past.

When I met this father at a conference, I could scarcely believe my eyes and ears. Beside me was a radiant man whose strength was quite literally found in the "joy of the LORD" (Nehemiah 8:10). As might be expected, he spoke of the past with hesitation; to share the sensitive details of personal tragedy cannot be done easily or flippantly. But there was love in his voice, radiance on his face, and optimism as he spoke about the future. In fact, he was scheduled to share in different churches how God had transformed a person who was a bitter, defeated failure into a victorious, Spirit-filled disciple. One person who knew him well said, "The apostle of bitterness is now the apostle of love."

How does God take a Christian who lives one-half inch from hell and make him live one-half inch from heaven? It's not easy. There is a price to be paid. The divine Surgeon must be permitted to use His scalpel to cut, cleanse, and break so healing can take place. In fact, such spiritual surgery is more painful than physical surgery. God does not use an anesthetic; He does not do His work while we are asleep. God can take any brokenhearted believer and make him or her a radiant, loving person. But when He performs such heart operations His children are wide-awake.

He often begins by prying us loose from our misguided notions of what being yielded to God means. Shorn of our superficiality, we are finally forced to accept the drastic treatment we really need.

Let's consider some of the shallow notions of what commitment to God involves. Then we will be more ready to see how God changed an apostle of bitterness into an apostle of love.

CLEARING THE GROUND

Perhaps the most widely held misconception within the evangelical community is the belief that yielding to the will of God involves little more than standing in a dedication service to sing "I Surrender All." Countless defeated Christians have responded to such appeals without any measurable results. Yet such believers have conned themselves into believing that they are yielded to God because they responded to a challenge to follow Christ. Perhaps they are; perhaps not.

There are several basic weaknesses in many so-called dedication services. Often we are challenged to do something heroic for God, for example, become a missionary, give more money, or witness to our neighbors. We are told (and in a qualified sense this is true) that God wants strong, courageous Christians who can weather the difficulties of life and emerge unscathed. Young people are challenged to do more for God (one youth leader says God wants "gutsy"

Christians). Consequently, those who respond to a "challenge" determine that they will witness for Christ, reject the attraction of the world, and be dedicated Christians.

The difficulty with such an approach is this: it often appeals only to natural, human inclinations. The challenge to be different, to witness, or become a missionary can be accepted without the slightest understanding of the power of the Holy Spirit or what commitment to Christ really means. Consider: hundreds of young people leave well-paying jobs and go to other countries with the Peace Corps. Every cult in the world has committed followers who are willing to accept a life of poverty and, if necessary, die for its cause. Even political activists who espouse no religion are often willing to work sacrificially for their stated goals. If we ask people to dedicate themselves to the Christian cause, we often are simply employing the same motivations used by sects all over the world. And this, I believe, is why most so-called dedication services have little or no effect on the Christian community. It is not a lack of sincerity but a lack of understanding that is at stake. Perhaps this is why one Christian, after dedicating himself to God countless times, borrowed a line from *Alice in Wonderland* to describe his spiritual experience: "I have to run real fast just to stay in the same place!"

Of course, God does want us to be willing to be missionaries, to witness, and to be courageous. But as we shall see, these qualities are the by-product of a more radical transformation God wants to do in our hearts.

Our misunderstanding of true commitment might explain why thousands of halfhearted Christians are under the comfortable illusion that they are dedicated to God. They have all the right credentials to prove it: they go to church, give a percentage of their income to missionaries, and for the most part stay out of trouble. They might be dedicated to the cause of Christ and yet be controlled by purely human motivation. As Charles Spurgeon once said, "Some Christians are healed before they are wounded; they are clothed before they have seen their nakedness." Consequently, they may be oblivious to their true spiritual condition.

How do we make progress in surrendering fully to the will of God? Let's consider that now.

BEGIN WITH SIN

Firmly entrenched within every human being lies a most deceptive presupposition, namely, that circumstances and other people are responsible for our responses to life. "If only my son had not murdered my wife . . . if only the people within the church had accepted me . . . if only . . ." So reasoned the man referred to earlier, who spent a decade a half-inch from hell. But when God began to close in on him, he came to an inescapable conclusion: bitterness is always sin, regardless of how many cruel circumstances crush us or other people fail us. There was no way for him to be delivered from the nightmare of the past without calling his bitterness *sin*.

This man could have stood in a hundred dedication services, prayed an equal number of prayers for God's help, and still be the victim of uncontrollable emotional trauma. The unvarnished fact is this: God does not accept excuses for sin.

Whenever we can pinpoint sin in our lives, we are on the way to true spiritual progress—after all, there is an excellent remedy for sin! But it is not enough simply to confess our sins (although confession is all that is necessary for forgiveness) if we want to be delivered from sin's power. We must go a step further and accept the fact that God also has a remedy for the sin nature within us. Confessing our sins is often like sawing branches off a tree; but if we do not want the tree to grow, it is more effective to strike at its roots. That is why God, the divine Surgeon, is not concerned only that we confess our sins; He goes directly for our hearts.

We cannot appreciate this until we see how helpless we are to change our inner motivations and emotions. We cannot overcome bitterness by making a New Year's resolution. "This year I will not be bitter." God has to show us how destitute we are apart from Him. Sometimes He does this by our study of the Scriptures, but often the lessons of Scripture must be reinforced by the ugly tragedies of life. The man who lost his wife at the hand of his son made a revealing statement: "For ten years I was strong and defeated; now I am weak and victorious." Did you get that? To be strong in ourselves is defeat; to be helpless in ourselves makes us candidates for God's power.

I've known "successful" Christians who have not learned that lesson—Christians who have gone as missionaries, witnessed to others, and yet have lived defeated, albeit dedicated lives. The call of the Peace Corps, cults, and political revolutionaries is to the strong, the courageous, and the shrewd. The call of God is to the weak, the helpless, and the broken. In Christianity the strong are defeated, the weak are victorious. As Paul said, "When I am weak, then [not two weeks later] I am strong" (2 Corinthians 12:10). To respond to a heroic challenge is relatively easy, but to accept the words of Christ, "Apart from me you can do nothing" (John 15:5), is difficult. I doubt whether any one of us knows how spiritually hopeless we are apart from Him. No wonder we need the Holy Spirit to show us how bad off we really are.

Perhaps now we can understand why so many people who pray "Lord help me" never receive the help they expect. They want the Lord to take their fleshly (that is, carnal) abilities and add to them His power, making them strong enough to cope with the difficulties of life. But our selfish motivation is so abhorrent to God that He will not do that. He is not in the business of helping the humanly strong become stronger; rather He takes the weak and makes them strong *in Himself.*

This is why failure can be a steppingstone if we respond to it in the right way. Anything that helps us see ourselves as the rebellious sinners we really are is a help. When the mask of self-righteousness has been torn from us and we stand stripped of all of our accustomed defenses, we are candidates for God's generous grace. When God takes us apart piece by piece, we identify with the pain Paul felt when he cried, "I know that nothing good dwells in me, that is, in my flesh" (Romans 7:18). If it takes a hundred failures to learn that, it is worth it. Because apart from that experience, we never make any spiritual progress. On God's scorecard this truth is a square one.

What next? Once we have confessed our sin and admitted our helplessness, we must accept as true that statement of Paul, "We know that our old self was crucified with him in order that the body of sin might be brought to nothing, so that we would no longer be enslaved to sin" (Romans 6:6). This is God's remedy for the self-life (that is, the part of me that wants to be in control instead of God).

Here is what we must do: we must realize that Christ won a legal victory over our selfish nature when He died on the cross. I cannot crucify my old nature, but Christ can and did. Now the victory He won can be applied to me by a deliberate act of faith, that is, by accepting His victory as mine.

This does not mean that we will not have our sin nature anymore; it is not a matter of saying, "I've arrived!" No, it is the beginning of being free from slavery to myself and to humanly uncontrollable desires. Without this act of faith in Christ's victory, we will always be controlled by the forces of sin. A life of victory and fulfillment will always be a mirage in the middle of an endless desert.

How could a man who was the victim of such tragedy be delivered from bitterness and depression? "I got on my knees," he recalls. "I confessed my sin, which I had justified for so long—then I accepted the fact that Christ had already won the victory for me."

With eyes still hot with tears he went to those whom he had resented to ask their forgiveness. He was finally a free man.

Does it happen overnight? Sometimes. This man was changed so suddenly because he was so desperate. But for most of us it takes time. The Bible says we are to "grow in grace." Our faith becomes stronger as we study the Scriptures and mature spiritually.

Christ has pried all of our excuses from us; His victory is great enough for any failure—it is good for broken hearts of all shapes and sizes. As the once bitter man put it, "For years I underestimated what Christ can do!"

Have you?

A NEW COMMITMENT

Once we have come this far, we are ready to commit ourselves—our past, present, and future—to God. The word *commit* means to deliver into another's charge. It involves transferring the responsibility for your life to another Person.

When South Vietnam fell to the rule of the Viet Cong, hundreds of people wanted to flee from the armies that ravaged the countryside. Thousands fled to airfields and seaports hoping to escape the coming disaster. When some families saw that they could not leave, many mothers gave their babies to men aboard a ship. They did this hoping that their children would be better off being with strangers than suffering starvation, war, and death. That was surely the most pathetic sight I have ever seen on television. Think of it. Mothers committed their children to people they did not know. They parted, knowing full well they would never see those children again.

This tragic story illustrates two facts about commitment: (1) the mothers trusted the judgment of those (in this case, strangers) to whom they gave their children; they believed others would do what was best for the children; and (2) there was no possibility of having their children back—the act was final. Quite apart from how they would feel about it in the future, the transfer of authority had been made.

What does it mean to commit ourselves to God? For one thing, it is an act of faith. It is the belief that God is well qualified to take care of what we give to Him. Fortunately, we do not have to commit our lives to Someone whom we do not know or to a Being who does not know what is best. Paul had every reason in the world to believe that God was able to keep that which he had committed to him (2 Timothy 1:12). If God does not know what is best for us, who would? Certainly not ourselves, since our knowledge is so fragmentary and distorted. Can you be sure you will be alive for another five years? Can you guarantee five minutes? Only God, who knows the future and understands the implications of eternity, is a trustworthy guide.

Also, our commitment is not based on feelings. To return to the sad plight of the Vietnamese mothers: regardless of how they felt later, the outcome could not be changed. Feelings had nothing to do with the commitment once it was made.

Many people give themselves to God, only to feel that their burdens are back on their own shoulders once again. They repeatedly give themselves to God and are engulfed in the slough of despair. But commitment to God is based on the One to whom the commitment is made—not on the feelings of the one who makes the commitment. Speaking of this, Henry Teichrob wrote:

> A shareholder does not lose his place in the corporation because he feels tired or ill or even unhappy. His benefits in the corporation rest on the fact that he is a shareholder. His "commitment" to the corporation provides the benefits as a shareholder. The fact of the matter rather than the feelings, determines the outcome.[1]

Our commitment to God is not taken back just because we feel that the burden is back upon our own shoulders. Once we have given a matter to God, that commitment is not nullified by the fluctuations of our emotions or the bitter struggles of personal experience.

LIVE FROM THE INSIDE OUT

What does it mean to be filled with the Holy Spirit? Does it mean that we smile all the time? Should we expect that all who walk in the Spirit should look alike, act alike? No.

To walk in the Spirit is to have Christlike responses to the experiences of life. The fruit of the Spirit essentially involves our attitudes toward the many and varied situations we all face. To be controlled by the Spirit means that we are not controlled by what happens on the outside but by what is happening on the inside.

Recall once more that man who experienced a decade of failure. He says, "I've learned that no man can make me hate him!" What he means is obvious—the most bitter experiences of life need not make us bitter; the most obnoxious individuals need not make us resentful. The power of God within enables us to accept the circumstances without.

And how do we walk in the Spirit? Like committing ourselves to God, it is an act of faith. It is not a matter of the way we feel or whether we have had an indescribable experience. "The righteous shall live by his faith" (Habakkuk 2:4).

We do not have to beg the Holy Spirit to control us— He delights in doing so. The reason He indwells those of us who are Christians is that His fruit, the fruit of the Spirit, might blossom in our lives. The only obstacle that blocks the ministry of the Holy Spirit within us is sin. Paul urged us not to grieve the Holy Spirit, and in the same context gives a list of sins that rob us of spiritual power—anger, bitterness, and gossip, to name a few (Ephesians 4:28–32). If our lives are free of known sin, we can begin each day by committing ourselves to God and anticipating the guidance of the Holy Spirit. We need never think that we have to overcome the Spirit's reluctance; He has been freely given to us in order that He might control us.

We must choose to depend on the Holy Spirit for power, just as we depend on Christ's death for forgiveness. We all know that the basis of our forgiveness is Jesus Christ's death on the cross; similarly, the basis of the gift of the Holy Spirit is Christ's ascension (John 7:39; Acts 2:33). Just as we receive forgiveness by faith, and we prove our faith by thanking God for Christ's death, so we accept the ministry of the Holy Spirit by faith and thank God for Christ's glorification. Forgiveness and the work of the Holy Spirit are both accepted by saying thank you to God.

Let me illustrate it this way. If you bought a two-volume book and carelessly left one volume at the store, what would you do when you got home? You would return to the store and get the other volume. Since you paid for both, you need not be content with just one. Similarly, salvation has two aspects—one is forgiveness and the other is the ministry of the Holy Spirit. Both have been provided, paid for. We experience them by faith in saying thank you to God for what He has *already* done.

Remember this: the Holy Spirit is more willing to control us than we are willing to let Him. He will empower any believer who is willing to remove the obstacles to spiritual growth and begin each day with faith in the Spirit's presence and ministry.

Failure helps us learn these lessons. The key question is whether we are prepared to pay the price that God demands to turn our failure into success. That price is admitting our failure, repenting of the sin that causes it, and applying the cross to our sinful nature. Only then can we live a committed life and walk in the Spirit once again.

What God did for a bitter, defeated man, He can do for us all. Why not let Him, just now?

CHAPTER 10

BUT I'M SO MESSED UP

A divorce shatters all family relationships. The wife feels hurt and cheated; the husband is often bitter against his ex-wife. Children are treated like pawns on a chessboard.

No one knew this better than a certain woman reared in a remote village. She had married well, she thought. As a new bride, she dreamed about the security and happiness her marriage would bring. Perhaps her expectations were unrealistic; perhaps she was too preoccupied with her own ambitions to recognize the first signs of tensions in her marriage.

After a few initial arguments, she and her husband hoped they could reconcile their differences. But the tensions between them mushroomed. Eventually they agreed that they could not live together any longer. The decision was agonizing but, from all appearances, necessary. They were divorced. Only those who have lived through the trauma of divorce can understand this woman's anguish.

True, divorces are common. But their increasing number does not lessen the hurt. This woman was so deeply grieved that she felt she could never share her life with someone else again.

But time heals all wounds, or at least lessens the pain of the initial blow. After she had pulled herself together emotionally, she eventually met a man who seemed to have all of the qualities her first husband lacked. Rather than face the future with loneliness and insecurity, the woman accepted the man's proposal. *This* marriage would be a success.

Despite this optimism, her second marriage showed signs of strain. At first the irritations were manageable. The woman dared not let herself think that this marriage would end like the first. Yet, the foundations of their relationship began to crumble. Patching up their differences was like trying to support a teetering building with wallpaper. Something fundamental was wrong; the resources needed to make this marriage work were lacking. Before long, the end was in sight. The result, a second divorce.

Some women would have buried their frustrations in their career. They would have relocated in another city, gone back to school, or learned a skill. But this woman could not. Her family believed not only that a woman's place was at home but that the woman was to be obedient to the whim of her husband. Furthermore, in her locality, no jobs were available to women. All she knew—all she could know—was the household chores, the drudgery of the routine.

It is not surprising that the decision to marry again was made easily. But now, the woman was bitter, angry at God, and disgruntled with men. This time she married without even calculating the risk. If her marriage didn't work, another divorce would rescue her from the bonds of her meaningless vows. She was crushed by guilt and filled with resentment.

She was married for only a short time. Predictably, she experienced a third divorce.

Then a fourth.

Then a fifth.

Any further marriage vows would have been a mockery. Since chastity was no longer an option, she decided not to bother with the formality of another wedding. When she met the sixth man, they decided to live under common law.

And then? Then she met Jesus Christ.

The story is told in John 4:1–30.

Her confrontation with Christ was quite accidental, so far as she was concerned. It began as just an ordinary day for this woman, another day to ponder her meaningless existence. At noon she left her home to trudge a quarter of a mile to get a bucket of water at the town well. In the background was Mount Gerizim; to her right was Mount Ebal.

From a distance she saw a man sitting at the well. As she came closer, she recognized that He was a Jew.

"Give me a drink," the man said.

The woman was startled. She knew the hostility of Jews toward the Samaritans, who were a mixed race. How could this man stoop to drink from *her* vessel?

"How is it that you, a Jew, ask for a drink from me, a woman of Samaria?" she asked.

Ignoring her question, the man directed her thoughts to another topic: "If you knew the gift of God, and who it is that is saying to you, 'Give me a drink,' you would have asked him, and he would have given you living water."

Living water? The man did not even have a bucket! How could He draw water from this deep well? How could He promise *living* water? Was He as great as Jacob who had dug the well? Hardly.

But the woman was wrong. This man *was* greater than Jacob. Or, at least, He claimed to be. "Everyone who drinks of this water will be thirsty again, but whoever drinks of the water that I will give him will never be thirsty again. The water that I will give him will become in him a spring of water welling up to eternal life." The words flowed from His lips.

The woman listened incredulously. But the man spoke with such assurance that she was willing to test His promise. "Sir, give me this water, so I will not be thirsty, nor come all the way here to draw."

What a relief, if she would not have to carry water from the well each day! But Christ did not offer her water like that in Jacob's well. He did not come to eliminate physical and temporal needs. He came to supply the deeper need of spiritual thirst.

In order for the woman to grasp His offer, He said, "Go, call your husband, and come here."

With embarrassment, the woman replied, "I have no husband."

Christ, nodding in agreement, added, "You are right in saying, 'I have no husband'; for you have had five husbands, and the one you now have is not your husband. What you have said is true."

How did He know this? She'd never seen Him before. The woman suspected that He might be another Jewish prophet. So she said, "Our fathers worshiped on this mountain, but you say that in Jerusalem is the place where people ought to worship."

Christ's reply was startling. He did not tell her she must go to Jerusalem to worship, as the Jewish leaders insisted. Rather, He said, "Woman, believe me, the hour is coming when neither on this mountain nor in Jerusalem will you worship the Father. . . . But the hour is coming, and is now here, when the true worshipers will worship the Father in spirit and truth, for the Father is seeking such people to worship him. God is spirit, and those who worship him must worship in spirit and truth."

God was not pleased with either the worship at Gerizim or Jerusalem. He looked for real worshipers, those whose hearts wanted fellowship with Him.

Standing before Christ was a woman who had had five unsuccessful marriages and was presently living in adultery with a sixth man. Morally, her life was beyond repair. Was there any hope for her? Christ offered her forgiveness. And He suggested that she was one whom the Father was seeking to be a worshiper.

GOD IS SEEKING WORSHIPERS

It is odd that we should so often forget why God made us. We busy ourselves with earning money and cram our spare moments with pleasure. We talk glibly about "serving the Lord" and being busy for Him. But often we forget that such matters are secondary; they are the by-product of true worship. And if we haven't learned to be worshipers, it doesn't really matter how well we do anything else.

What does the Father seek? Missionaries? Pastors? Generous laymen? Christ taught that the Father seeks worshipers. *Worshipers* satisfy His desires. *Worshipers* please Him. Are *you* a worshiper?

Consider the familiar verse: "But if we walk in the light, as he is in the light, we have fellowship with one another, and the blood of Jesus his Son cleanses us from all sin" (1 John 1:7). This does not merely mean that if we walk in the light we have fellowship with other Christians: it means that if we walk in the light we have fellowship with God, and He has fellowship with us. We and God have fellowship one with another.

We not only have the privilege of having fellowship with God, but *God desires to have fellowship with us!* He seeks our fellowship. He seeks our worship.

How selfish we are! We often go to church to see what is in it *for us;* we read the Bible so *we* will receive a blessing; we pray so that God will fulfill *our* wishes; we look to God to supply *our* needs. Everything (our church, devotions, and service) is judged by how it profits us!

Isn't it time we reversed our priorities? Isn't it more important that God be satisfied than that we are? If God seeks worshipers, should we not learn (if we don't yet know) how to worship Him in spirit and truth? Is this not more important than teaching Sunday school, witnessing, or tithing?

Often Christians ask, If God already knows our needs, why should we have to ask Him for anything? Consider George Macdonald's reply:

> What if he knows prayer to be the thing we need first and most? What if the main object in God's idea of prayer be the supplying of our great, our endless need— the need of Himself? ... Hunger may drive the runaway child home, and he may or may not be fed at once, but

he needs his mother more than his dinner. Communion with God is the one need of the soul beyond all other need: prayer is the beginning of that communion.[1]

In other words, the reason we must ask God for things He already intends to give us is that He wants to teach us dependence, especially our need for Himself.

God is looking for worshipers. And if the religious elite are too proud or too busy to learn to worship Him, He seeks the worship of those whose lives are trapped in moral ruin. Perhaps they, like the woman of Samaria, can more readily appreciate God's forgiveness; perhaps they are better candidates for two-way fellowship with the Creator! The Father seeks such to worship Him.

THE ELEMENTS OF WORSHIP

Christ's statement gives us the clue to what worship involves. First, it is not confined to geographical location. The Jews worshiped at Jerusalem; the Samaritans worshiped on Mount Gerizim. Yet, Christ said the time had come when people would worship God neither at Jerusalem nor at Gerizim. Worship does not happen because of correct geography.

How often Christians assume they have worshiped God simply because they have been in church. We are told that the church building is "God's house" (an inaccurate designation borrowed from the Old Testament Temple) and conclude that worship *must* take place there. Not necessarily. God was not pleased with the worship at Jerusalem (the Holy City). Neither is He impressed with beautiful cathedrals.

Are you ready for this? It is possible to attend church regularly, participate in the service, and not worship God at all. Worship isn't listening to a sermon, appreciating the harmony of the choir, and joining in singing hymns. It isn't even prayer; for prayer can be the selfish expression of an unbroken heart.

Worship goes deeper. Since God is Spirit, we fellowship with Him with our spirit; that is, the immortal and invisible part of us meets with God, who is immortal and invisible.

Prayer may be worship; singing may be worship; reading the Scriptures may be worship—but not necessarily.

Second, we must worship in truth, without hypocrisy or any form of dishonesty. The people in Isaiah's day were not condemned because they sang the wrong songs; neither did God judge them because they prayed unorthodox prayers. They even brought the prescribed sacrifices. Were they worshiping God? Here is Christ's answer, quoting Isaiah: "Well did Isaiah prophesy of you hypocrites, as it is written, 'This people honors me with their lips, but their heart is far from me; in vain do they worship me, teaching as doctrines the commandments of men'" (Mark 7:6–7). The content of their prayers did honor God. They did bring the prescribed sacrifices. But their hearts (their spirits) were far from God.

What goes through your mind when you attend church? Do you wonder how your clothes compare with those of the person next to you? Are you self-conscious, anxious to make an impression on those you meet? Do you anticipate the end of the meeting so that you can greet your friends? Do you find it difficult to concentrate on what's going on because you are day-dreaming about business or pleasure? If so, *you have not met God.* You have honored Him with your lips, but your heart is far from Him!

The greatest commandment is not "Thou shalt not commit adultery," neither is it "Thou shalt not bear false witness," nor even "Thou shalt not steal." These are needful, but the greatest commandment—the most important—is, "You shall love the Lord your God with all your heart and with all your soul and with all your mind" (Matthew 22:37). If our greatest desire—our real ambition—is not to love God, we are not pleasing to Him. Period.

Finally, Christ taught that the Father *seeks* worshipers. That seems odd! Would not all people—especially Christians—want to worship the Father? Would it not be more appropriate for us—the creatures—to want to meet the Creator? That might be more appropriate, but that is not the way it is! The Father, the almighty God, does the seeking. And my guess is that there are relatively few who respond.

The reason? Many of us are not thirsty for God because we have quenched our thirst at other fountains! Consider God's word to Jeremiah: "For my people have committed two evils: they have forsaken me, the fountain of living waters, and hewed out cisterns for themselves, broken cisterns that can hold no water" (Jeremiah 2:13). They forsook the fountain of living water and drank from man-made cisterns.

Thirst must be quenched! If our desires are not met by God, we will quickly find something else to alleviate our thirst. And when we become satisfied with stagnant water holes, the more difficult it is to seek the fresh stream.

To change the figure of speech slightly, if we are not nourished by the bread from heaven, we will satiate ourselves with crumbs from the world. And once we have become addicted to the world's nourishment, our appetite for God is spoiled. Many of us are so satisfied with ourselves that God's request for worship appears to be an intrusion. We don't like to interrupt our schedules to seek Him.

For example, we have become addicted to affluence.

A professor in a leading evangelical seminary remarked that the greatest difficulty with the men who came to study was that they had been reared in middle- or upper-middle-class homes. As a result, they had never learned to trust God for anything tangible. They were reared in homes where there was always enough money for food and clothes.

Few of us have ever had to pray in sincerity, "Give us this day our daily bread." We have never needed God quite that desperately. And if we have never had to trust God for earthly things, we find it more difficult to trust Him for heavenly things.

We've also absorbed the world's love of pleasure. Paul predicted that in the last days people would love pleasure more than they love God (2 Timothy 3:4). That day is here. Consider this: Are we as willing to go into debt for the work of God as we are for a vacation to Hawaii? Are the pleasures at God's right hand as appealing as a promotion or unexpected salary increase?

Repeatedly, God warned the Israelites that bumper crops and productive gardens would turn them away from Him (Deuteronomy 6:1–12). Their history as well as ours has confirmed one fact: *it is almost impossible to develop true worshipers in affluent surroundings.* Recall Christ's words about how hard it is for the rich to enter the kingdom of heaven. Who needs God when there are no pressing emergencies? Why should we take the time and effort to know Him when we are doing so well by the strength of our own hands?

We are puzzled as to why the saints of the past had such a passion to seek God, when we sense no such need ourselves. Martin Luther prayed as much as three hours on days that were especially busy; Hudson Taylor and John

Wesley did the same. Such devotion can't be understood by those who pay their respects to God on Sunday and find no special need for Him during the week.

It was in exile as slaves in a foreign land that the sons of Korah sang, "As a deer pants for flowing streams, so pants my soul for you, O God" (Psalm 42:1). Seldom have we been that thirsty!

Although God seeks worshipers, we continue to use Him for selfish ends. He is prayed to in emergencies, and His Son is used to forgive our sins. But we are satisfied with that much. We want a religion that is convenient, one that demands a minimum of our time and effort.

But those who have drunk deeply of the living water discover that the world's fountains are but muddy water holes in comparison. Malcolm Muggeridge, a distinguished English journalist, in his book *Jesus Rediscovered* wrote,

> I may, I suppose, regard myself [as] or pass for being, a relatively successful man. People occasionally stare at me in the streets—that's fame. I can fairly easily earn enough to qualify for admission to the higher slopes of the Internal Revenue—that's success. Furnished with money and a little fame even the elderly, if they care to, may partake of trendy diversions—that's pleasure. It might happen once in a while that something I said or wrote was sufficiently heeded for me to persuade myself that it represented a serious impact on our time—that's fulfillment. Yet, I say to you—and I beg you to believe me—multiply these tiny triumphs by a million, add them all together, and they are nothing—less than nothing, a positive impediment—measured against one draught of that living water Christ offers to the spiritually thirsty, irrespective of who or what they are.[2]

Did you understand what Muggeridge was saying? He is famous, wealthy, and influential; yet, these triumphs, if multiplied by a million, are still nothing in comparison to "one draught of that living water Christ offers to the spiritually thirsty."

Remember Beth, described in chapter 1? She probably will never serve God in public; she likely will never have a successful marriage; even her good name may be lost forever. Success (as we often think of it) is no longer a possibility for her. Is there anything she can do to please the Father? Yes!

The invitation Christ gave to the woman of Samaria includes Beth, and it includes you and me. Worship is possible even for those who are victims of an unhappy marriage or crushing emotional experiences. It's a possibility for us all. *Those who truly worship, truly serve.* The Father seeks such to worship Him.

CHAPTER 11

A FORMULA FOR ACCOMPLISHMENT

I was gifted with a vivid imagination. Reared in a rural area, I had ample time to think about the future. Sometimes I imagined I was a businessman, sometimes an airplane pilot, sometimes an evangelist. One persistent characteristic of my daydreams was this: regardless of the vocation I chose, I was always a smashing success!

Of course, I realized that these escapades of my imagination could never come to be—at least, not all of them could! But I cherished the hope that those dreams would become reality. For the most part they haven't.

This discrepancy between the ideal (what we imagine

ourselves to be) and the real self (what we actually are) causes conflicts. The middle-aged are especially prone to experience deep disillusionment. For many years they have visualized themselves as a success, but now their dreams may be far from fulfilled. As one man put it, "I'm forty-five. I thought I would have it made by now, but what has happened? I am where I started, if anything, a bit further back." He passed his prime without the achievement he wanted.

Even greater disappointment comes to many people in their sixties. They have saved money faithfully for their retirement and have made starry-eyed plans about what they will do with their leisure time. Now that they have reached the "paradise" of retirement, they are either too lonely or too sick to enjoy it. It's like patiently following a rainbow only to discover that there is no pot of gold at the end!

Looking back, I realize that I am not nor shall I ever be the person I visualized in my youth. I've had to accept my limitations and realistically evaluate my gifts.

I'm not complaining. I've had the opportunity to attend several schools, teach in Bible school, pastor a church, and do some writing. But my daydreams were unrealistic. Most of them will never come to be.

Perhaps this is the way it should be. For God has been trying to teach me that we don't have to do everything we had planned to do; we don't have to reach all of our goals in order to qualify for "success" in His eyes.

In fact, it is often when we are striving to reach our goals (even valid ones) that God breaks into our lives and reorganizes our priorities. Soon we learn that His notion of success differs from ours.

Let me explain. I was busy accomplishing my goals, earning graduate degrees, preaching, teaching, and writing.

I was so busy that I scarcely had time to ask God to rubber-stamp my plans! Of course, theoretically I wanted to do these things only for Him. But a rather insignificant incident changed the direction of my life.

A Christian man in California had a sign on his desk that read, "You may not be accomplishing as much as you think you are." That observation began cleaning the cobwebs out of my mind. Here I was, doing more than most other Christians (or so I thought). But I couldn't shake the suspicion that that sign spoke the truth about me. Inwardly, I knew that my activities were not as significant as I thought them to be. God could do without me. He didn't need me to accomplish His work in the world. True, I was busy. But I began to suspect that I wasn't doing much for God.

Then another incident happened. I was hospitalized for a week for what I had mistakenly taken to be a heart attack. I began to reflect over my life. If I died today would I have any regrets? What would I do differently if I knew I would die within one year? Or ten?

I was forced to reevaluate my priorities. What did God want me to do on earth? What was He seeking? Educated Christians? "Successful" pastors? Popular writers? No. At least, these are not number one on His list. He was seeking worshipers! He was looking for men and women who knew Him. "The people who know their God shall stand firm and take action" (Daniel 11:32). In fact, the Scriptures teach, "The eyes of the LORD run to and fro throughout the whole earth, to give strong support to those whose heart is blameless toward him" (2 Chronicles 16:9).

Obviously, the activities we do *for* God are secondary. Above all else, God is looking for people who long for communication with Him. That's why Paul said that he counted everything but dung (KJV) that he might know Christ (Philippians 3:8–10). J. I. Packer observed that when Paul says these words, he not only means that he considers his past accomplishments as worthless but also that he does not live with them constantly in his mind. Packer asks, "What normal person spends his time nostalgically dreaming of manure?"[1] Paul's single passion was to know Christ. He didn't want anything—even his prized achievements—to detract him from this goal.

Now, since I wasn't accomplishing as much as I thought I was, since my ministry was something less than spectacular, I decided to try an experiment. It was this: rather than have my activities rotate around myself and my ministry, I would sincerely attempt (not just verbally, as I had done countless times before) to make my life rotate around God. In other words, He would be brought from the fringes into the very center of my life.

Remember Copernicus? He was the astronomer who rejected the theory that the planets rotate around the earth. He found it difficult to explain planetary motion according to this scheme. So he proposed a new theory, namely, that the sun is the center of the universe. With this theory, he found that the motion of heavenly bodies could be more easily explained.

I knew I needed my own "Copernican revolution." Until now, my world was at the core of my life. God was worked in only when needed. Now I decided that He would be on center stage, and my world—schedules, sermons, and exams—would rotate around Him. This, of course, necessitated some adjustments.

WORKING ON THE SPECIFICS

The first practical problem was *time*. Although in theory I had always put God first, no one would have guessed it by looking at my schedule. The spare moments I used for Him were wedged between other deadlines. Now some adjustment was necessary. I began by blocking out forty-five minutes of each day for one purpose: to know and worship God. I decided it wouldn't even matter whether God would answer my prayers. In fact, my requests were cut to a minimum. These forty-five minutes were not for me, they were for *Him*.

How do we begin to honor the Almighty? I took my cue from Psalm 50:23: "The one who offers thanksgiving as his sacrifice glorifies me." In the New Testament, it is put this way: "Give thanks in all circumstances; for this is the will of God in Christ Jesus for you" (1 Thessalonians 5:18). Throughout the Bible there are scores of direct references to praising God. Worship (which is our response to God's revelation) always produces praise.

So after a brief time of confession, I would begin to thank God for His attributes. Then I'd recount all the blessings that He gives us in Christ (there are at least thirty). I thanked Him for excellent health, my family, my schedule, and my irritations. In short, I thanked Him for everything except sin.

The more I studied the Scriptures, the more I realized that this was a dimension of worship I had been neglecting. David said, "Bless the LORD, O my soul" (Psalm 103:1). This does not mean that mortal man can bless the immortal God. Our thanksgiving (which is a response to God's blessing) is often referred to in the Old Testament by the same word as the blessing itself. To bless the Lord means to praise Him for His blessings! The rest of Psalm 103 is a magnificent il-lustration of how God is honored; it is by recounting His attributes and goodness to His people. Anyone who wants to can glorify God! "The one who offers thanksgiving as his sacrifice glorifies me."

Second, I knew that God was pleased with His Word. "I bow down toward your holy temple and give thanks to your name for your steadfast love and your faithfulness, for you have exalted above all things your name and your word" (Psalm 138:2). God's promises are backed by the honor of His name.

In fact, there are at least two (perhaps more) promises of success in the Scriptures. In each case the formula is the same. To Joshua, God said that if he would meditate in the book of the law day and night and be careful to do all that is written in it, "Then you will make your way prosperous, and then you will have good success" (Joshua 1:8). The same promise is given in Psalm 1 to those who meditate in the law of God day and night: "He is like a tree planted by streams of water that yields its fruit in its season, and its leaf does not wither. In all that he does, he prospers" (v. 3).

I realized I would have to readjust my thinking habits to meditate continually (or, at least, more often) in the Scriptures.

So I determined to think (in an unhurried way) about several verses each day. I was surprised at how often I had read the Bible without "seeing" (and it *does* take observation) how much of it applied to me. Previously, I had memorized whole chapters of the Bible, but often I had never thought of the significance of what I quoted. Now, with my mind sufficiently free of stray thoughts, God was teaching me truths I had not experienced before. I began to learn a startling truth—namely, that I didn't know as much as I thought I did! Progress was slow (and still is), but gradually I found that concentration on the Word was possible—and meaningful.

Along with my praise and Bible study, I would often read a devotional book or spend time in evaluating my life. But I tried to keep the focus primarily on God's honor, rather than merely presenting Him with a list of needs, although I sometimes did that, too.

I had determined to try this experiment and continue it whether it "got results" or not. That is, I was not looking for spiritual power, great answers to prayer, or spectacular blessings. For a change I hoped to honor God without asking, "What's in it for me?"

Perhaps you have guessed what happened. I kept my appointments, prepared sermons, and did some writing— and everything became easier. Did not Christ say that if we seek first the kingdom of God and His righteousness that many other things would be added unto us? I realized what I had always known theoretically: that time spent with God is not wasted. A man who is chopping a tree is not wasting time when he sharpens his ax! The woodcutter who is too busy to sharpen his ax loses in the long run.

Isaiah put it vividly: "But they who wait for the LORD shall renew their strength; they shall mount up with wings like eagles; they shall run and not be weary; they shall walk and not faint" (Isaiah 40:31).

A RETURN TO BASICS

My new approach to Christian living taught me several lessons. I was a bit surprised to discover that God had been, in many ways, a stranger to me. Maybe that's why it is so difficult for some of us to trust God in a crisis: we are forced to commit ourselves to Someone we don't know very well. Of course, we cannot know God fully, and we certainly cannot understand all His ways. But learning about Him in the Scriptures and then talking to Him directly develops the trust relationship, and without faith it is impossible to please Him (Hebrews 11:6).

A poem by Nancy Spiegelberg vividly describes the experience of those who determine to know God better:

> *Lord*
>> *I crawled*
>> *across the barrenness*
>>> *to You*
>>> *with my empty cup*
> *uncertain*
>> *in asking*
>>> *any small drop*
>>> *of refreshment.*
> *if only*
>> *I had known You*
>> *better*
> *I'd have come*
> *running*
> *with a bucket.*[2]

Isn't that true of us all? If we knew God better, we could trust Him for more. If we understood that we were created for fellowship with Him, we'd spend more time fulfilling that purpose. I've begun to learn that fellowship with God leads to faith; it develops trust.

Although we become Christians instantaneously by faith in Christ, knowing God and developing faith is a gradual process. The simple fact is that some Christians know God better than others. There are no shortcuts to spiritual maturity.

It takes time to be holy.

I also realized that the best motivation for spiritual maturity is not the prospect of freedom from sin but the prospect of knowing the living God. Of course all forms of sin must be condemned. But people will face up to their sins only when their appetite for God is aroused.

Teenagers don't leave their bicycles until they want a car; beggars don't leave their crumbs until they are offered a ham sandwich. Similarly, sin is unattractive only when seen next to genuine two-way fellowship with the Creator.

All of us know "average" Christians who are glad they accepted Christ's forgiveness, but they mistakenly believe that this is all that Christianity is. They believe that a Christian is simply a sinner minus his (or her) sins. They've never experienced anything beyond that. Consequently, church is boring, reading the Bible is a chore, and praying is a waste of time. (None of the above is as exciting as football, for instance.)

The answer? It's not merely to condemn carnality but to develop a thirst for something better. Until we've known by experience that the pleasures at God's right hand are better than the pleasures of the world, we won't change our lifestyles.

Another thing happened to me. I found myself less concerned about my reputation as one who is "successful." God's approval became more important than that of my friends. Of course, I am still conscious of other people's opinions and, for that matter, conscious of my reputation. But I can rejoice more easily when others are more "successful" than I. I've begun to play the game for the Coach rather than the unpredictable applause of the fans.

Remember the story of the disciples who were elated with

their success? They came to Christ and announced, "Lord, even the demons are subject to us in your name!" Christ replied, "Nevertheless, do not rejoice in this, that the spirits are subject to you, but rejoice that your names are written in heaven" (Luke 10:17, 20). God has had to slap me across the face for rejoicing in the wrong things! Slowly I'm learning that my joy must be in God and not in what He allows me to accomplish.

Finally, whenever I missed my appointment with God, I noticed it immediately. "Oh, taste and see that the LORD is good! Blessed is the man who takes refuge in him!" (Psalm 34:8). My appetite for God was increasing. And just like skipping meals, skipping my appointment with God created hunger. As Christ said to the lukewarm Laodicean church, to those who would let Him in, "I will come in to him and eat with him, and he with me" (Revelation 3:20). Two-way fellowship with the Lord of the universe! That's enough to whet even the most carnal taste buds. Is it any wonder that meeting God is more satisfying than being introduced to the famous people of this world?

When a Christian dies, we often say, "He went to be with the Lord." I know what we mean. But unfortunately that expression might betray a shallow understanding of our relationship with God *now*. Paul said that we *are* in Christ—crucified, buried, risen, and seated with Him in heaven (Ephesians 2:6). That means we are as close to God as Christ is; we are already "with the Lord." Death brings only a different kind of relationship. But our proximity to God will never be closer than it is now, and He is available for fellowship. Are you?

If you are like me, you will never reach all of your goals. Your "real" self will never match your "ideal" self. Face that fact. Don't live in a dream world, thinking of what you *could* have done or even *should* have done. Success, as we usually think of it, is simply not an option for everyone. But fellowship with God is! And if the chief end of man is to know God and enjoy Him forever, *that* goal is possible for you. Try it. You can't go wrong.

After all, you may not be accomplishing as much as you think you are!

CHAPTER 12

WHEN IS IT TOO LATE TO BEGIN?

The best years of my life are over. I've made my share of mistakes. I'd give anything to relive it, but it's gone forever. Should I bother beginning *now?*" The man who said these words had buried his wife a few weeks earlier. Theirs had not been a happy marriage. He and his wife squabbled about the relatives and about their children. Throughout the years, his wife had depended more on her mother than on him. He in turn was not strong enough to be the leader in his household.

The sins of the past affected the next generation. The children had suffered. The hurts and insults of the past could not be changed. It was too late to talk to this man about what he *should* have done. As Shakespeare observed, "What has been done cannot be undone."

But what about the future? Is there still an opportunity to live a meaningful life, a chance to work in God's vineyard? Any possibility for rewards at the judgment seat?

If we were asked to set up a reward system for believers, we would probably work out a detailed merit scale. Those who sacrificed many years serving God would receive a large reward; those who served for a short time would receive a small reward. Naturally, we would try to be fair to all.

Surprisingly, Christ taught that God doesn't give rewards that way. He told a parable that on the surface is puzzling. In fact, it seems that God is unfair.

In Palestine, the grapes ripen toward the end of September, and after that, the rains begin to fall. If the harvest is not gathered in quickly, it is ruined. Any worker is welcome, even if he can only do an hour's work.

Christ taught that the kingdom of heaven is like a land-owner who went out early in the morning to hire workers. Those who began at nine o'clock agreed to work for one denarius. Other workers came at twelve noon and some as late as five o'clock.

Here is the surprise: when they lined up at the end of the day to receive their wages, *everyone* received the same—one denarius. As might be expected, the first group grumbled, "These last worked only one hour, and you have made them equal to us who have borne the burden of the day and the scorching heat" (Matthew 20:12). Imagine paying employees equally without even checking their time cards!

Perhaps the most obvious lesson from this parable is that seniority in the kingdom of heaven does not imply superiority.

We will not be judged by how long we serve but by *how* we serve. For example, some Christians die in their youth. If rewards were based on the number of years of service, they would never have a chance to be rewarded like the veteran workers.

God is generous! These men did not all do the same work, but they did receive the same pay. Think of how good God is. He gives us the physical, mental, and spiritual ability to work in his kingdom, and then He rewards us for doing it!

The landowner (who represents Christ in the parable) says to the complainers, "Am I not allowed to do what I choose with what belongs to me? Or do you begrudge my generosity?" (Matthew 20:15). We might resent seeing our friends receive wages for something they didn't do. We might become especially irritated if we did more and received less. But God delights in giving, and if we are envious of others, it shows that we have missed a basic lesson in living the Christian life. More of that later.

A second observation is that quantity is not as important as quality. Remember Paul's words in 1 Corinthians 3? Some Christians spend their lives accumulating wood, hay, and stubble, all of which will be burned in the day of judgment. Others have gold, silver, and precious stones that will endure the test. A few gems held in the hand are worth more than a gigantic pile of rubble!

You see, it is possible to work for Christ just as a non-Christian works for his company. We can serve with selfish motivation or for personal fulfillment. All such work, though done in God's name, will not receive God's approval. The distinction is whether we have served out of gratitude to God and dependence on Him or whether we worked with purely human motivation.

One mistake made by those who came to the vineyard at nine o'clock in the morning was this: they worked for what *they* could get out of it! They didn't lift a finger until they "agreed" (probably some haggling went on) with the landlord for a denarius a day. They wanted to know what was expected of them and what they could expect in return.

This group of workers were like students who want to know how many classes they can cut so that they can be sure to use their quota! They were like Christians who want to know whether to tithe on their net or gross income so they don't have to give more than expected!

Notice also their critical attitude. They grumbled because they were envious at what others received. Self-righteously, they reminded the landlord, "[We] have borne the burden of the day and the scorching heat" (Matthew 20:12). They looked with pride on their own accomplishments; they forgot that no man (in God's kingdom) is accepted because of his sacrificial achievements.

God doesn't "pay" us because we have worked for Him. We are given rewards (which we don't deserve) because He is generous! We see this principle clearly in salvation, but we don't always see it in the Christian life. We all admit that we will be in heaven solely because of God's grace. But we forget that any reward we get will be because of God's grace, too.

It's not a matter of saying, "Lord, I've served you for thirty years, I will expect thirty crowns!" No. God has the right to give us whatever *He* wishes, and if He gives *nothing*, that would be fair, too. Remember, God owes us nothing. *Whatever* we get is because of God's goodness.

A third observation is already obvious: the first group of workers didn't realize that serving the keeper of the vineyard (Christ) carries its own reward. The second and third groups of workers did not agree to work for a certain amount. They left that up to the landowner, believing that he would do whatever was right. They were just glad for the chance to work in his vineyard.

Working for Christ, out of sheer appreciation for what He has done, is in itself the highest privilege. The one who comes to the vineyard late is to be pitied because he didn't have the thrill of spending his entire life serving the Lord. But even for him, there will be reward—a *generous* reward— at the end of the day.

Too late to begin? Never. God is still hiring workmen, even those who are of retirement age! Remember, no one has to be unemployed in God's vineyard.

WHERE TO BEGIN?

Perhaps you are one who has come to work in the kingdom at five o'clock. True, the hour is late. How much better if you had worked in the Father's vineyard all the day. Whether you are a Christian who had spent your life in the "far country" of selfishness or are an unbeliever who has never known the Keeper of the vineyard, realize this: *it is better to show up for work in the kingdom of heaven at sunset than not to show up at all!*

If in the end you should receive a reward, it will be because of God's grace; but then those who receive rewards for working all day will receive their reward on the same basis.

Where should you begin? We've become so accustomed to judging ourselves by our performance (and this is not all wrong) that we forget that in God's books, what we *are* is more important than what we *do*.

God's will is that we be conformed to the image of Christ

(Romans 8:29). In practical terms, that means that God wants to develop the same character traits in us as exist in Christ. We are to react to the situation of life as Christ did.

Of course, this does not mean that we simply roll up our sleeves and determine to live differently. The radical purity of heart that God demands—the rich qualities of love, joy, peace, and patience—are not the product of practice. Rather, they are supernatural characteristics that are developed by dependence on the Holy Spirit (Galatians 5:22–23).

It is a deadly error to suppose that the Christian life can be lived by sheer willpower, abstaining from a given list of sins or fitting into an expected mold. Once we have understood the deep change God wants to bring about, we will see that His demands are so great that only He can supply what He demands! In short, living an acceptable Christian life requires constant fellowship *with* and dependence *on* the living God.

That is why those who have failed miserably are often the first to see God's formula for success. Those who believe they are doing well, often the ones who are faithful in their "work" for the Lord, are the last to appreciate their need for the Holy Spirit's constant power. Most autobiographies of "successful" godly men and women confirm this truth: those who (figuratively) went to the highest mountains also experienced the deepest valleys. In fact, you can't have a mountain without valleys! It is the broken and the contrite heart that God does not despise.

What next? God always wants us to be involved with people. Paul was getting anxious to die and be with Christ, which was far better, but then he realized that it was better still that he live a while longer. Why? Because he could be a blessing to others and encourage them in the faith (Philippians 1:23–26). Our responsibility is to show love to all people in *specific* actions of kindness. Those who offer someone a cup of cold water in the name of the Lord will not lose their reward.

Perhaps you are an invalid in bed. Why not phone a friend and tell him that you will pray for him constantly? Or why not write some letters of encouragement to missionaries or lonely friends? "Truly, I say to you, as you did it to one of the least of these my brothers, you did it to me" (Matthew 25:40).

Recently, during a trip to Washington DC, my wife and I visited the Tomb of the Unknowns at Arlington National Cemetery. After World War I, the American government had the bodies of four unknown soldiers brought to Washington. Then Sergeant Edward Younger arbitrarily selected one of these four to be buried where the Tomb of the Unknown Soldier would be built. On the tomb are inscribed these words: "Here rests in honored glory an American soldier known but to God."

As I stood there, I realized that all of us will die as unknowns. We may be remembered by our friends, but succeeding generations will forget us. Even today, of the 180,000 graves in Arlington, tourists visit only a few, such as John F. Kennedy's, his brother Robert's, and the Tomb of the Unknown Soldier.

As the years pass, the names of many heroes are obliterated from the minds of men. Yes, we die as unknowns. And when that happens, many things we thought important will be irrelevant. All that will remain is what will not be burned up at the Bema, the judgment seat of Christ, those things that have the dimension of the supernatural. The rich qualities of faith, love, and joy that Christ gave us are all that will survive.

What should we be doing today? We should be discovering the power of a personal God in an age that rejects the supernatural. Then others who see us will not pity us because we are Christians. They will discover that our lives defy human explanation.

God is at work completing His plan before His Son returns to the earth to wrap up history. He wants us to rise above the pessimism, despair, and cynicism of our age. He wants us to display the presence of the supernatural, to rejoice always, pray without ceasing, and in everything give thanks.

It's never too late to begin!

CHAPTER 13

SHEDDING THE GRASSHOPPER COMPLEX

A man who was losing his memory went to his doctor for advice. He received this diagnosis: "We cannot help your memory without impairing your eyesight. The choice is yours. Would you rather be able to see or to remember?" The man thoughtfully replied, "I would rather have my eyesight than my memory. I'd rather see where I am going than remember where I have been!"

This story (which is probably apocryphal) reminds us of something we need to hear: at this present moment, our future is more important than our past. We have no claim on the past, but we do have a claim on the future. The past is closed; the future is yet open for new possibilities. But we cannot live meaningful lives in the future if we are tied to the failures or successes of the past. Paul was an example for us all: "But one thing I do: forgetting what lies behind and straining forward to what lies ahead, I press on toward the goal for the prize of the upward call of God in Christ Jesus" (Philippians 3:13–14).

A basic prerequisite for progress in the Christian life is to learn from the past without being controlled by it. Many Christians are "hung up" on their past. They have tried and failed and are determined never to try again. Their past performance is their excuse for present impotence. If they could choose, they'd prefer their memory to their eyesight. They are blinded to the possibilities of the future because of the memories of the past. Paul reminds us that sometimes it is better to forget than to remember.

But let us assume that you have the assurance of God's forgiveness; suppose that you realize that God is willing to make the best of your past. You want to change the direction of your life. Now what? How should you face the future? How do you tackle your hang-ups? Here are some necessary steps.

First, *consciously include God in every aspect of your life.* Remember the story of the Israelites at Kadesh-barnea? Twelve men were sent to spy out the land of Canaan. They found the land to be productive, just as God had promised. But ten of the twelve spies were shaken with fear, the fear of failure. The Canaanites had walled cities; the Israelites were accustomed only to tents; furthermore, there were "giants" in the land, the sons of Anak.

The result? The majority report read, "We seemed to ourselves like grasshoppers, and so we seemed to them" (Numbers 13:33). The Israelites were small, the Canaanites were giants; the Israelites were open to attack, the Canaanites lived in fortified cities. Conclusion: failure is inevitable. *Grasshoppers don't win wars.*

Notice that when the spies saw *themselves* as grasshoppers ("We seemed to ourselves like grasshoppers"), it was then they assumed that the Canaanites thought of them as grasshoppers, too ("And so we seemed to them"). Of course this wasn't true! The Canaanites were scared of the Israelites because rumors of Jehovah's power had reached them (Joshua 2:9–11).

But when you see yourself as a grasshopper, nothing— not even obvious facts—makes the slightest difference. The "grasshopper complex" is the most crippling of all psychological attitudes.

Perhaps the greatest single sin of Christians in any century is the mistake made by the spies: *facing human problems with human resources.* Whether it is preparing a church budget, deciding to share our faith, or tackling our personal problems, the question often is, How much can *I* do? As a result, perpetual failure is inevitable. Instead of comparing our problems with God, we compare them to ourselves. Little wonder we soon feel like grasshoppers (or, at best, pygmies) among an army of giants.

Christ's disciples were guilty of the same sin of unbelief. When Christ suggested that the multitude be fed, Philip checked their resources and concluded, "Two hundred denarii worth of bread would not be enough for each of them to get a little" (John 6:7). The best Philip could do was to match human resources with human needs. The result: there was simply not enough food to go around.

The boy who gave his lunch to Christ saw the same problem, but apparently, he had enough insight to include

Christ in his calculations. Maybe Christ could go beyond human resources; maybe He could do the supernatural; maybe He was relevant to pressing problems. The boy was right.

Why did the spies succumb to the "grasshopper complex" at Kadesh-barnea? First, it began with negative thinking: "We are not able to go up against the people, for they are stronger than we are" (Numbers 13:31). The spies thought of more reasons why they couldn't do it than why they could. Second, they exaggerated the situation: "We are like grass-hoppers." Unbelief always distorts the facts. A Christian who refuses to trust God for problems as they arise will magnify his difficulties. A pessimist is not only well aware of the negative side of every circumstance but also invents added reasons why failure should be expected.

Third, the next step of unbelief was their desire to return to Egypt (Numbers 14:2–3). People who haven't experienced God's power constantly hover between their faith in God and their desire to succumb to the world. As James reminds us, "A double-minded man [is] unstable in all his ways" (James 1:8). Fourth, they became ignorant of God's will. The next day they decided to conquer the land by themselves. What was the result of this foolish decision? Without God, they were beaten as easily as grasshoppers (Numbers 14:44–45).

All of these disastrous consequences followed because ten men looked at themselves and concluded that they could not cope with the situation. Perhaps they reasoned, "Sure, God is with us, but we have to be realistic!" Maybe they even thought that their attitude displayed humility: "Who are we to think that we can achieve such victory?" But God was angry with them. Why? Because they did not compare the cities and the giants with God; they only compared these obstacles with themselves.

Undoubtedly, God often puts us in situations that are too much for *us* so that we will learn that no situation is too much for *Him*. Goliath was stronger than David; the Midianites were stronger than Gideon; and the storm on Galilee was beyond the control of the disciples. But neither these problems nor ours are too difficult for God.

Do you consciously include God in *all* your plans? Do you face the future with optimism, knowing that nothing is too hard for the Lord? Or is your life characterized by *human* abilities, *human* responses, and *human* resources? Only those who learn to expose each new situation to the living God are delivered from the curse of the grasshopper complex.

Second, *choose a specific difficulty in your life and trust God to conquer it.* Many people who have either psychological or emotional problems do so because they have skeletons in their closet, skeletons that they have tried to hide from others and from God. The trauma of asking others to forgive them or the fear of repeated failure has filled them with pessimism and resentment. But those who are prepared to face themselves with their weaknesses and fears can be freed from such bondage.

Wes Pippert, who for years worked as a Washington-based reporter with United Press International, said that early in life he was afraid of most things. He made a rational decision to acknowledge the fear and proceed to do everything he was afraid of. The result was emancipation. He no longer was afraid, or he had consciously decided to disregard his fears.[1]

Think of what troubles you most at this moment. Your hot temper? Your inability to love others? Are you afraid that your children will go astray? Do you fear the future? Face those problems directly by giving them to God. "Casting all your anxieties on him, because he cares for you" (1 Peter 5:7).

The Scriptures teach that all of the spiritual battles that we face have already been conquered by Christ on the cross (Colossians 2:15). God is honored when we simply say "Thank You" for what Christ has already done. If the Israelites had taken God at His word, they would have realized that Canaan was already theirs (Joshua 1:3). It was simply a matter of acting in faith. Canaan could have been theirs if they had believed that God does not deceive His people.

Let me repeat. Choose the difficulty that troubles you the most. Trust God either to remove it, or, if it is not sin, trust God to give you the grace to accept it with joy. If you act on your own, you'll be as easily routed as the Israelites. But if God be for us, who can be against us?

Third, *don't become content with too little; ask God for new areas of ministry and experience.* Even if you think of yourself as a "victorious" Christian, choose to meet even greater challenges. It is heartbreaking to see many Christians who are either content with failure or content with using only a fraction of their potential. This book was written to help those who have failed, which includes all of us to a greater or lesser degree. Failure is not God's plan for us! Neither does He want us to live below par. The Israelites were more content to wander in the wilderness than they were to tackle walled cities. Such sinful contentment, which always leads to discontentment, is the result of unbelief.

Remember Caleb? He was not easily satisfied. At the age of eighty-five, he might have been pardoned for wanting a small home next to the seashore and a garden in the backyard. After all, he had already participated in many victories; why not let someone else conquer the new territory?

Is he content with that? No, he wants to conquer the

mountain God promised him. So he takes the city of Hebron with its Anakims and fortified walls (Joshua 14:12–15). Here was a man who believed that God specialized in victory, not defeat. He was not afflicted with the grasshopper complex.

True, we should be content with our surroundings and our lot in life (Philippians 4:11), but we should never be content with our experience of God's power. Like Paul, we should press on toward the goal for the prize of the high calling of God in Christ Jesus (Philippians 3:14).

Ask God for a mountain! Ask Him for the wisdom to see new challenges that can only be met with His help. Perhaps He wants you to tell your neighbor about Christ; maybe He wants you to have a ministry of encouragement; or He might want you to change the spiritual atmosphere of your home. *Trust God for something that only He can do!* You'll be amazed at the results. "For the eyes of the LORD run to and fro throughout the whole earth, to give strong support to those whose heart is blameless toward him" (2 Chronicles 16:9). God calls us to live lives we cannot live, so that we must depend on Him for supernatural ability. We are called to do the impossible, namely, to live beyond our natural ability. Someone has said, "If you've never been called to the impossible, you haven't been called."

I've always liked the prayer of Jabez: "Oh that you would bless me and enlarge my border, and that your hand might be with me, and that you would keep me from harm so that it might not bring me pain!" (1 Chronicles 4:10). Here was a man who did not feel guilty about asking God to bless him and enlarge the influence of his life. And because he asked this for God's glory, Scripture assures us, "God granted him what he requested." Don't be satisfied until you have seen God conquer the unconquerable!

Fourth, *have a positive rather than negative approach to life.* Many Christians refuse to develop a positive attitude. The reason is simple: they *plan* to fail. Athletic coaches often notice that a player will develop what J. K. Summerhill called a "loser's limp." A player sometimes develops a limp in order to have an excuse for not doing better. Without the limp, he would have to bear the responsibility for incompetence, but with it, he believes that he can't be blamed for a poor performance.

Many Christians constantly complain, "You can see how badly I am handicapped by_____." They would be floundering in bewilderment if their handicap were suddenly removed! Their weakness, whether it be their personality, appearance, lack of ability, or difficult circumstances, has been their security; it provides the rationale for their failure. The truth is they do not want to exchange their pessimism for optimism. They choose to emphasize the negative rather than the positive so that they have a ready-made excuse for not making the grade. They assure us that they have already lost the race even before it has begun.

How can we overcome the "loser's limp"? It is by determining that each day will be a challenge to let God display His power. I've found that my best mental preparation for a positive attitude is to begin each day reminding myself of God's promises. Here are a few: "For nothing will be impossible with God" (Luke 1:37). "We know that for those who love God all things work together for good, for those who are called according to his purpose" (Romans 8:28). "I can do all things through him who strengthens me" (Philippians 4:13). Of course, there are many more such promises. Reminding ourselves of them gives us the proper perspective on life.

After you have recited these promises, thank God for everything—your trials, blessings, and challenges. Thanksgiving is a sign of trust; if we believe that all things work together for good, we will be able to be thankful in the most depressing circumstances. Paul's advice is basic to our victory: "Give thanks in all circumstances; for this is the will of God in Christ Jesus for you" (1 Thessalonians 5:18).

Even if you don't *feel* particularly thankful, thank God for your blessings in Christ (e.g., forgiveness, acceptance, and righteousness), and your attitude will change. I've found that the most difficult struggle is to begin to consciously thank God for all things; then when I think of all God's blessings, my second difficulty is to know when to quit.

Try this right now. List as many blessings as you can, and thank God for each one. In a few moments you will view your problems from a different perspective and face life more objectively. God wants us to be optimists, not pessimists; He wants winners, not losers.

Fifth, *learn to encourage other Christians.* Consider the following statements: "I am the subject of depression of spirit so fearful that I hope none of you ever get to such extremes of wretchedness as I go to . . . personally, I have often passed through this dark valley [of depression]."

"I was very melancholy, I may say, on Saturday evening. The old scenes reminded me of my ministry, and this accompanied with such regret for past failures."

Who spoke these words? Carnal Christians who were living with one foot in the world? A new convert who didn't understand the basis of God's acceptance? Hardly. The first statement was made by one of the world's greatest and most successful preachers—Charles Haddon Spurgeon. The second is recorded in the diary of Andrew Bonar, an outstanding saint and friend of Robert M'Cheyne.

The point is obvious: everyone—including the greatest

saints—experiences regret, unbelief, and the reality of failure. Remember what we said earlier: even successful Christians experience varying degrees of failure. If we compare ourselves with Christ, there isn't much difference between us.

We are all cut from the same piece of cloth. No matter how successfully we may hide our problems, we are still much the same *inside*. Bible records and church history reveal to us that many of God's servants have at times handed God their resignation.

Paul wrote that God "comforts us in all our affliction, so that we may be able to comfort those who are in any affliction, with the comfort with which we ourselves are comforted by God" (2 Corinthians 1:4). God expects us to use *our* failures and *His* comfort to be a help to others. Spurgeon could be a blessing to thousands of people because he knew and understood despair. On a less spectacular level, we can be an encouragement to others by sharing our failures and our victories with them. One of my great encouragements was to become friends with those who were personally acquainted with A. W. Tozer. This man, who knew God so intimately, had days when he was so discouraged he felt he could not continue as a minister. Imagine! A man who instructed thousands in the deep things of God often felt he was a miserable failure. He, too, was made of flesh and blood.

If Tozer felt he was a failure, maybe it's not so surprising that we feel that way too. He needed encouragement. So do we.

The most persistent problem in the church is discouragement, and if we do not freely commend people for what they are, they will simply say, "What's the use"—and quit.

A minister, who resigned from his church because of utter discouragement, was inundated with reports of blessing—at his farewell. The people did not want to see him leave; they testified of his effective ministry among them. If they had done that a year earlier, they could have rescued a man from the slough of despondency.

Do you want to make a lasting impact on someone's life? Find a lonely or discouraged Christian. Listen to his needs and tell your personal struggles to him. Your honesty may be as refreshing as a cool stream on the great Sahara. Pray together. Remember, your problems are destined to help us help others.

Let me repeat the fifth step: learn to affirm and encourage the lives of others. As a by-product of encouraging others, you will strengthen yourself. Mutual fellowship produces individual blessing.

Finally, let the words of Peter Marshall become your motto: "It is better to fail in a cause that will ultimately succeed than to succeed in a cause that will ultimately fail."

Better to love God and die unknown than to love the world and be a hero; better to be content with poverty than to die a slave to wealth; better to have taken some risks and lost them than to have done nothing and succeeded at it; better to have lost some battles than to have retreated from the war; better to have failed when serving God than to have succeeded when serving the devil. What a tragedy to climb the ladder of success, only to discover that the ladder was leaning against the wrong wall!

God specializes in the impossible. When we positively accept His grace, our failures can be turned into success. Only a big God can do such big miracles. Isn't it time we shed the grasshopper complex? After all, God specializes in success, not failure. "He raises the poor from the dust and lifts the needy from the ash heap, to make them sit with princes, with the princes of his people" (Psalm 113:7–8).

NOTES

Chapter 9: There Is a Price

1. Henry Teichrob, "The Committed Way," *Brigade Leader* (Fall 1973): 19.

Chapter 10: But I'm So Messed Up

1. C. S. Lewis, *George Macdonald: An Anthology* (New York: Macmillan, 1948), 51–52.
2. Malcolm Muggeridge, *Jesus Rediscovered* (New York: Doubleday, 1969), 61.

Chapter 11: A Formula for Accomplishment

1. J. I. Packer, *Knowing God* (Downers Grove, IL: InterVarsity, 1973), 21.

2. Nancy Spiegelberg, in *Decision*, November 1974. ©1974 by the Billy Graham Evangelistic Association. Used by permission.

Chapter 13: Shedding the Grasshopper Complex

1. Wes Pippert, "Ambition, the Ethics of Success," *His* (February 1975): 31.

MORE BOOKS BY ERWIN W. LUTZER

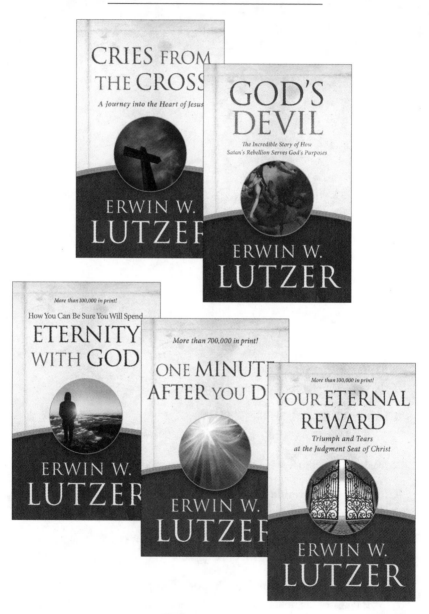

CRIES FROM THE CROSS
A Journey into the Heart of Jesus
ERWIN W. LUTZER

GOD'S DEVIL
The Incredible Story of How Satan's Rebellion Serves God's Purposes
ERWIN W. LUTZER

More than 100,000 in print!
How You Can Be Sure You Will Spend ETERNITY WITH GOD
ERWIN W. LUTZER

More than 700,000 in print!
ONE MINUTE AFTER YOU DIE
ERWIN W. LUTZER

More than 100,000 in print!
YOUR ETERNAL REWARD
Triumph and Tears at the Judgment Seat of Christ
ERWIN W. LUTZER

MOODY Publishers™

From the Word to Life

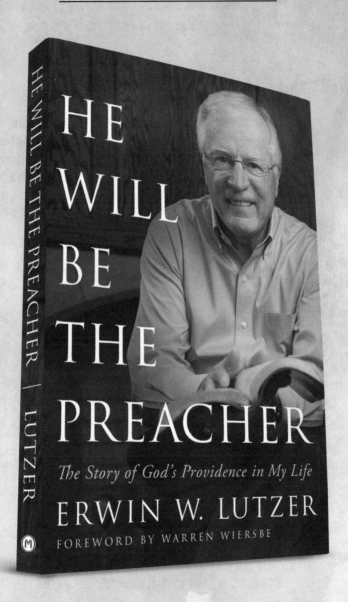